THE
EASTERN
EUROPE
COLLECTION

PRESIDENT MASARYK TELLS HIS STORY

Karel Čapek

ARNO PRESS & THE NEW YORK TIMES
New York - 1971

Reprint Edition 1971 by Arno Press Inc.

Reprinted from a copy in
The Newark Public Library

LC# 71-135797

ISBN 0-405-02739-7

The Eastern Europe Collection
ISBN for complete set: 0-405-02730-3

Manufactured in the United States of America

PRESIDENT MASARYK
TELLS HIS STORY

T. G. Masaryk.

PRESIDENT MASARYK
TELLS HIS STORY

Recounted by
KAREL ČAPEK

Translated from the Czech

NEW YORK
G. P. PUTNAM'S SONS
1935

FIRST PUBLISHED IN
THE UNITED STATES
IN 1935

TRANSLATOR'S FOREWORD

THIS account of President Masaryk's life was taken from his own lips and set down in his own words by Karel Čapek. The chapters were not told consecutively as they are given here; they have been built up from material gathered by Čapek during several years of intercourse with the President. For weeks at a time Čapek stayed with President Masaryk and his family in their charming country house at Topolčanky, in Slovakia; and in the course of talks on summer days in the fields, beside a bonfire in the evenings, on quiet afternoons in the rose-covered summer-house, or on picnics which the whole family joined, he learned the facts, events, and theories which he has woven into this book. Often he would absent himself from the party, while he wrote down and arranged what he had heard the previous day, reappearing later, the plan of the work fresh in his mind, to draw the conversation round to some point which he wanted amplified or elucidated.

Thanks to Capek's ingenious and careful mosaic-work, we have here a unique self-portrait of a man whom his country honours as teacher, philosopher, and leader, and whom we know as the maker of a State.

D. R.

CONTENTS

PRESIDENT MASARYK TELLS HIS STORY

THE WAR AND AFTER

CHILDHOOD

CHILDHOOD

Home

MY earliest memories. . . . They are just disconnected pictures. Once—I must have been
about three years old—I saw a runaway horse at
Hodonín; it went galloping down the street;
people jumped out of its way in all directions; only
one little child fell under its hoofs, but the horse
sprang over him and he was not hurt at all. That
remains fixed in my head. Then I remember, about
that time, how my father in Mutenice used to snare
crows, and all kinds of wild beasts and birds. I
remember too how—in Mutenice—I would go to
the schoolmaster and ask him for pencil-ends, and
I scribbled with them before I had learned to write.

My home was the country round about Hodonín;
it was all the Emperor's estates there, and so
wherever my father, who began life as a coachman
on these estates, was sent, we used to move with
him. When I was only two we moved from Hodonín
to Mutenice, where we stayed till the spring of
1853; then we came back to Hodonín and lived in
a cottage on the lake. Even to-day I can still see that
distant level stretch, and I think my childish impression has remained with me; that is why I love

the plains; mountains I like to see in the distance, but I don't care to live among them: the narrow valleys crush me, and there is so little sunshine. In the year 1856 we moved to Čejkovice on to a farm; two years later we had to go to Čejč for a year, then back to Čejkovice, and there we lived till 1862. In 1861 I began to go to the secondary school at Hustopeč; my parents returned to Hodonín, but in 1864 they were sent back to Čejč, and three years later they left the Emperor's estates and went into service with private people at Miroslav and on a farm called Suchohrdlý. After all this housemoving we settled at Klobouky, and stayed there from 1870 till 1882, and I used to go home there for the holidays. But the real home of my childhood was Čejkovice.

My mother had more influence on me than my father had; my father was gifted but simple, it was mother who ruled at home. She was born at Hana, but she grew up among Germans at Hustopeč; this made Czech difficult for her at first. She was very fond of her three young scamps; perhaps I was her pet, but the one who deserved it was really my brother Martin, the best of us all in character and the finest in mind, *anima candida*, as they say.

My mother was a wise and clever woman; she knew something of the world and had lived for some time in "the best society," though only in service—she had been cook in a gentleman's family at Hodonín; but they were fond of her there, and, later on, they used to come to her for advice and help in their difficulties. Out of her knowledge of this society grew the desire that her children should rise a little in the social scale; and besides she knew very well the wretched conditions in which the serving and working classes lived in those days. She wanted to make us gentlefolks—it was through her efforts that I was sent to school.

My mother was religious. She loved going to church, but she hardly ever had time for it; she had to slave for the family. I have heard her say: "*Herrendienst geht vor Gottesdienst.*" I thought of that later, when I came to understand the political rôle of the Church, and Feuerbach's theory that religion serves political ends. Instead of going to church, my mother used to say her prayers from the prayer-book; the book was full of pictures—I remember a picture of the crucified Christ with blood flowing from His wounds; that was her favourite. And I liked to look at it too.

My father was a Slovak from Kopčany; he was born in serfdom, and remained in it all his life. Compared with my mother he had little positive influence on me. He was naturally gifted, but had never been to school; at Kopčany he learnt to read a little from an old woman, a soldier's widow

15

to whom the parish entrusted this function—there was no school there at all. In exchange for a reading-lesson the children had to dig potatoes for her. So he was altogether natural, a countryman not a townsman; he lived close to nature, especially after he had gone on to the farm; understood outdoor life, observed it, and observed accurately—he had quite an exceptional sense of folk and country lore. To this day I remember how one day in March he brought home, snuggled in his coat, a young hare which he had found crouching in a horse's hoof-print; and then he told us in such detail, and in such a lively, interesting way, the whole life story of a hare!

Though he had no schooling, he liked to see me go to school and was not ashamed to study with me; of course he took his studies, like everything else, from a utilitarian point of view: what one got out of it. He was not religious, but he was afraid of hell, and now and then he went to church on Sundays. It was my mother who decided every-thing; he gave in to her even when he did not agree.

A long time afterwards, when he came to see us in Prague, he was only interested in the way horses were shod there, what kind of shafts and wheels did the carts and carriages have in Prague. The only sights which interested him in the palaces on Malá

Strána were the porters—in a couple of days he had got to know them all and used to go and chat with them. In a few days he had had enough of Prague and we could not get him to stay any longer—he wanted home, the village, the country!

I felt and noticed in my father the results of subjugation and enforced servitude; he served and worked without pleasure, because he had to; he doffed his hat to his masters, but he had no affection for them. On the Emperor's estates serfdom still existed *de facto* even after 1849. But imagine—my father had to ask for permission to send me to the secondary school! Those were my first impressions of the social order: some official on the estate would be surly with my father and I had to look out. I used often to wonder how I could pay them out for it and give them a good thrashing! When the "lords and masters" came for the hunting, they would leave their fur coats at our house, and you have no idea how much I longed to vent my childish rage on those fur coats. After the hunt they usually had a meal at the gamekeeper's cottage, and the servants threw out the remains to the villagers, who would fight over them. Once they threw out something, macaroni I think it must have been, and the villagers did not know what it was, and called it worms, but all the same they fought over it like beasts. Things like that remain fixed in my mind.

PRESIDENT MASARYK TELLS HIS STORY

The Children Amongst Themselves

We three boys were very fond of one another; but I had quite a different feeling for each of my brothers. Martin, the middle one in age—we were each two years apart—I not merely loved, I felt a strange respect for him; he was a dear fellow—trustful, open, unassuming. The youngest, Ludvik, I used to order about a good deal, make him run my errands and so on. Martin I always think of as an ideal boy.

We three did not play together—each went his own way. The comrades I had were older boys; I always liked to be with older people and listen to them. I was even on friendly terms with one or two of the grooms on the farm.

* * *

Yes, so I began to go to school at Hodonín—that was a German school—and then at Čejkovice. When I think of my first schoolmaster at Čejkovice I can still see those hands of his: such hairy, bony hands which he used to cuff us with. At home my father learnt how to write from me; while he was a coachman he still couldn't write, but later on in his life, first as bailiff and then as farmer, he found it necessary to keep a note of the work and workmen,

18

what they did and how long they worked. I had to write these occasional notes for him; I used to draw lines in his note-book and rule the necessary columns. You see, my father did not like work. He worked when he had to, like any other bondsman. Serfdom! there you have it: unwillingness and compulsion.

The village school-teacher during my early years was a poor fellow; his salary was not very large, so he eked it out by various kinds of clerical work, served in the church, sang at funerals, and went carol singing. At vintage-time we boys would go with a barrel from one wine-press to another and collect for "teacher," as much as each farmer would pour in; then, all the winter he kept the barrel in the schoolroom behind the stove, since he had no cellar, and the must fermented there. Really it was little better than pauperdom: a farmer, especially when he was a mayor or councillor, treated the school-teacher as no better than a pauper. And naturally the down-trodden school-teacher had not much authority over the children; so he walloped and walloped us—that was his most usual method of teaching. A slave always uses a slave's methods, and gets his own back where he can. Think what an advance is represented by the school of to-day! But it still has much which needs reforming before it produces independent, self-confident individuals with a plucky attitude to life. School reform is really also the reform of the teaching profession; that means raising their social standing and their level of culture. At present the teachers themselves are demanding University education; suppose we were to try how University-trained teachers could get on with the children. The chief qualifications are: to be fond of children, to be able to understand their way of thinking and feeling, which is concrete and graphic rather than abstract and scientific; to make the lessons graphic, and link the information to something of which children are aware, concretely, in their surroundings; and to make education as individual as possible. Far more thought should be given to the schools, and to teaching and education in general . . . and far more money spent than hitherto. In the development of the school lies the development of democracy.

*　　*　　*

A boy brought up in the country has a lot to learn. I should say so! Just count it all up! he must know how to whistle with his lips, between his teeth, with one finger, with two, and with his fist; then how to snap his fingers in two different ways; he must know all sorts of ways of fighting, how to stand on his head, walk on his hands and turn cartwheels; and above all how to run, that is the chief thing. Then a boy must know how to use a sling and a bow, shy a stone, ride a horse, crack a whip and a switch, climb any tree, catch crayfish and water-beetles, swim, light a bonfire, slide, toboggan, shy a snowball, walk on stilts, and a hundred and one other things. Once we began to dig a tunnel, we were going to run a train to and fro in it; where we were going to get the train from did not worry us at all.

Just count up the number of occupations a boy has; making pop-guns from quills or elder twigs; carving whistles from willow twigs or goose bones, and clarinets from cherry wood; making pipes from the stems of wheat or gourds; manufacturing a long bow—perhaps even a cross-bow with the notched lath from a roof—and arrows to go with it; then a rifle, sword, and helmet; making balls and tip-cats, carving toy water-mills and windmills, or even an Easter rattle. He must be able to tie Gordian knots, and plait finger rings, and whole chains out of horse-hair—it was a German boy who was living *au pair* in our village who taught us that. And to do all this a boy has only a tuppenny jack-knife. To possess a real pocket knife was the height of our ambition. Anyone who could, borrowed a file or chisel or axe from home, and carved and carpentered away. Every boy is a bit of an engineer.

Once I had a great longing for a *grumle* or jews' harp; this is a kind of musical instrument which the gipsies use, shaped rather like a small lyre with a metal tongue on which you blow while you twang with your finger. Well, I wanted a *grumle* of my own, and I begged a gipsy to make me one. "All right," said the gipsy, "but you must bring me some iron for it." I brought him a piece of iron which I picked up on the farm. "And now you must bring me some bread." So I gave him some bread, and then butter and eggs—I don't know what I didn't have to bring that gipsy! But I never saw the *grumle* after all!

We played all sorts of children's games, all of them out of doors. We used to play "soldiers," and especially at wars, and were anything but pacifists. Or else "robbers": I was the robber chief and the bailiff's son the chief of police; of course whenever I got the chance I gave him a good hiding.

A boy will always have his treasure-box, full of all sorts of things: coloured beans, buttons, marbles, peacocks' and jays' feathers, little cubes of broken tile, bits of coloured glass, a prism from a chandelier, perhaps a discarded lamp from the church, and other treasures. Boys have their business deals as well; they lend out beans at high interest, they swop them, sometimes even sell them for a farthing apiece.

CHILDHOOD

Of course before all these boyish occupations a country lad must first of all have helped mother in the house, and then father in the fields. I do not know from my own experience what sort of life the little girls lived, since we were quite apart. Once, when I must have been about eight, my mother took me with her to the fair at Šaštín. We slept at the house of the gamekeeper there, whom we knew; he had a little girl about my age; we were there two days, and we children played together from morning till night. When we went home again I missed her terribly.

City boys have not so many different kinds of games; perhaps scouting makes up to them for it nowadays. Children should be left to look after themselves a bit; a child brought up in the country is more inventive, independent, and practical; a town child often cannot sharpen its own pencil, and has no idea of learning to be handy. And on the whole not many accidents happen in the country; sometimes one may sprain a toe, sometimes, it's true, one may even get hit on the head with a stone. I can remember three serious accidents: once a boy fell from a poplar tree, fairly high, and they said that his chest was affected afterwards. One boy got poisoned with henbane when they were playing at horses and the other boys fed him with it; and one boy got drowned while out bathing in the lake. I was there when they brought him home, and saw how his mother knelt down by him and began in a crooning, tearful voice to intone all little Joseph's good qualities: "My dear little Joseph, how good you were, now I shall never scold you again," and so on. Later I read that this kind of wailing over and praising the dead is the custom of all primitive peoples.

A child feels quite clearly whether his elders are free or not, and on what terms they are with each other. American children are freer than those in Europe; they are more *naïf* and open in their ways with other children and also with grown-ups; they are not afraid of their elders, but perceive that they too are frank among themselves. That is the effect of a Republic and of freedom. People do not lie, and are not continually afraid of being cheated or harmed by one another; they do not fear each other. I like to watch the children nowadays and to chat with them; it seems to me that they are already more self-reliant and open, and I say to myself that they will grow up into a free people. A Republic, you know, is a very fine thing!

And here am I back again at the question of schools and teachers. It is the business of the teacher in the school to impress on the children the principles of republicanism, democratic freedom, and equality; he should be the children's comrade.

CHILDHOOD

His authority must rest on difference of age and on his superiority in all matters of knowledge, practice, and character. I noticed that the American children are on terms of greater *camaraderie* with their teachers than the children here—and that all their lives Americans keep pleasant memories of their teachers and schools. In our country children heave a sigh of relief when they leave school; and yet to get to know things is a delight to a normal child. The American teacher plays football with the boys without fear of losing their respect. A bureaucratic teacher would not go tobogganing or skating with his pupils—he would be afraid of a tumble which might destroy his dignity or authority. Between teacher and pupil, just as between official and citizen, we kept an artificial distance—a constraint, You only need more *sans gêne*, more heartiness, and you have real democracy. Comenius says that school is the workshop of mankind; school trains the child collectively as well as individually, it educates him for society and for democracy. I would rather hear, instead of those ancestor-worshipping songs: "Oh Czechs of old, heroes of old!" etc., a new song: "Come on, you Profs., come on, let's be democrats!" We have a few such professors already, and so much the better!

Of course the same thing applies to the family. Not the blind authority of parents, not the passive obedience of children, exacted with everlasting nagging and grumbling, but training by example.

The Child and His World

I took after my mother in being deeply religious. At Čejkovice I was server to our chaplain, Father Francis—Satora his name was—and I absolutely adored him; I was fascinated by his white collar and that tight-fitting black—what is it called?—the clerical gown with little round buttons all the way down from the throat to the feet. While I was serving Mass it seemed to me that Father Francis was like God and I was his angel; that was my greatest happiness. Much greater than when I was singing in the choir. Well, you know, I was also proud of being a server. Father Satora was a curious fellow, quite unbalanced, a typical Slovak from Bořsic. Sometimes he was an absolute fanatic, and sometimes it seemed as though he were tortured by doubts; he was not in the good graces of either the ecclesiastical or the worldly authorities. Once I heard women whispering about Father Francis and the schoolmaster's wife, who had just had a baby. I did not understand it and racked my brains in vain to see what it meant. And one Sunday Father Francis preached a sermon in which he said that even a priest was prone to sinfulness, and that folk

26

must not take example from his life but from Christ's life and the words with which He taught them. It was a kind of public confession; I could not understand it at the time, but that sermon gave me a lot to think about. Why should people not take example from his life? It was only when I was mature and looked back on my childhood that I understood this and other things.

In the course of time, through my reading and experiences, I became more critical of priests, and it began to dawn upon me that there is a difference between Religion and the Church; the priests themselves admit, when they teach us at school, that though the Church is a divine institution, yet she has certain human characteristics, unessential, changeable, and therefore differing according to nation and land. Of course the older I grew, the more of those worldly characteristics I seemed to come up against; but I have never had doubts about God and theology; I have always been an optimist.

In those days I was not able even to imagine that there could be any other faith. At Čejkovice I found an article about Russia in an old almanac; there was something in it about the orthodox Church, and you cannot think how upset I was by the information that there was another faith beside ours which had its pilgrimages, hermits, saints, and miracles. I was impressed at the time by the argu-

27

ment that there are more Catholics than Protestants and Orthodox Christians; but I was disturbed to find, on comparing, that there are even more Mohammedans and heathens.

I also heard that at Klobouky, not so very far away, there were some Calvinists; I made a special reconnoitring expedition there one fair-time and crept into the Evangelical chapel; I was terribly afraid that I should fall down dead or be struck by lightning as a punishment—but nothing happened. Those bare walls, the pulpit instead of an altar, that seriousness and simplicity, all made such an impression on me that it took my breath away. I had heard how the Evangelicals were reproached for not believing in the use of bells; but in those days Protestants were not allowed bells; it was only a hundred years after the Patent of Toleration that they received the right to have bells. It puzzled me that the Catholics should admit the Protestants to be more cultured, orderly, and thrifty; I racked my brains to think how that could be. And I pondered on the saying: "That lasts like the Calvinist faith." I could not solve these riddles then, but Protestantism disturbed me more and more, and irritated me somehow.

Then there were the Jews. I was afraid of them. I believed that they used Christian blood, so I would rather go several streets out of my way than pass a house where a Jew lived; their children wanted to play with me because I knew a little German, but I wouldn't. It was only later at school at Hustopeč that I became more or less reconciled to the Jews. Once we made a school excursion to the Palavske hills. While we were romping and getting into mischief after our dinner at the inn, one of our Jewish schoolfellows slipped away from us into the yard. I followed him out of curiosity; he had gone behind an open gate and was kneeling with his face to the wall, praying. I was ashamed, somehow, that a Jew should be praying while we were playing about. I could not get it out of my head that he had been praying as devoutly as we did, and that he had not forgotten his prayers, even for games. . . .

And you know, all my life I have tried to be careful not to be unjust to the Jews; that is why I am said to favour them. When did I overcome in myself the anti-semitism of the common people? Well really, in my feeling perhaps never, only in my reason; it was my own mother who taught me the superstition about the Christian blood.

Of course, as a child I didn't only believe in the things we were taught at school and church; my Catholicism was a kind of superstition, permeated with Slovak mythology. I believed in all possible and impossible sorts of spirits, and perhaps most of all in the "midday witch" and the "twilight witch"[1] and that was because I used to forget the time when I was out playing, and come home late to dinner and supper. *Hastrman*[2] was especially popular among the boys; nearly everybody, they said, had seen him, but there were great disputes about his appearance and the colour of his hair, beard, and clothes; witches played a big part too, and then death and the devil; we all heard *him* once in church when a man broke out in an epileptic fit during mass. Wizards worried me too, when I read about them. So I lived in a kind of dual, ambiguous spiritual world; I might call it orthodox and unorthodox at the same time. In the unorthodox one, among those superstitions and anthropomorphisms (one might really say paedomorphisms!) there was no system. The twilight witch, the *hastrman*, and the other beings and monsters were each as it were apart, without connection with the others—it gave me a funny feeling. I came to realize at last that they were superstitions, but the line between superstition and faith I could not see clearly, and I could not help believing in the superstitions; they were so firmly rooted and generally accepted. The curate taught us the Catechism at school, but he himself did not con-

[1] Witches who appear at noon and twilight respectively, and carry off naughty children.—TRANSLATOR'S NOTE.

[2] A kind of fresh-water merman.—TRANSLATOR'S NOTE.

tradict the superstitions. I might perhaps say that
the midday witch is the eerie silence of the noonday
hour, and that the twilight witch is the dusk at
vesper time; but a child's mind clings to these
"paedomorphisms"; a child loves the poetry of
myths. Of course the child is always being snatched
away from his poetry: one day when I got home
after the angelus had rung, mother threatened me
that the twilight witch was sure to get me one of
these days; the next I had to be out watching the
potato fields[1] till after dark, and I was afraid of
the twilight witch—why, you silly boy, there's no
such thing as a twilight witch!

Neither at school nor at home was there any
serious mention of the spiritual essence of religion;
I never heard that one can or should meditate on
religion. The religion of the people, like the symbols
and the whole cult, was very material, altogether
objective. That religion might also have subjective
elements never entered into anyone's head; religion
was the truth of God revealed, it was the com-
mandments of God and the Church, and was, as
Vincent of Lerina formulated it, *quod semper, quod
ubique, quod ab omnibus creditum est.* I used only
to speculate in those days on such exterior things

[1] When the potatoes have been dug, the country boys go and
steal a few to roast on bonfires after dark, so someone has to keep
watch till the potatoes have been gathered in.—TRANSLATOR'S NOTE.

as, for instance, which is the greater sovereign, the Emperor or the Pope? When I came up against the idea of the Holy Trinity, the incarnation of God in a human body, and other dogmas which I did not understand, I used to ask Father Francis about them, but I had to content myself with the stereotyped answer: that is a mystery. That word forbade discussion, but it left me unsatisfied. Religion was simply lived and practised, the Church's teaching was simply accepted. Of the Bible we only got to know what was in the school-books and what we heard in church; the Bible was not read at home; only the Prayer Book some-times.

Some time before this one of the stable-boys at the castle hanged himself in the stable. Afterwards I was shown the little gate from which he hanged himself, and I can tell you that I was absolutely terrified of that little gate. I used to look at it with a kind of horror, and I would never cross the threshold of that stable. It seemed to me frightful and in-comprehensible to take one's life! Just try to realize what it means to take one's own life! It seemed to me so unnatural, so perverse! The thought remained at the back of my mind, especially later on when I found a book about people who continued to endure life in the most terrible situations; for instance, there was a certain monk who is said to have been

buried in the crypt, but he was only dead in appearance; he woke up, and had to wait till a new burial
released him, or else kill himself; he lived for
twenty years underground, feeding on the insects
which fell through the little window of the crypt
and drinking the moisture from the walls and
tombs. I could not help wondering, however, what
happened in the winter, when there are no insects;
but the casuistry of that example and others like it
laid hold of me, and impressed on me this problem
of voluntary death. My book on suicide is an
answer to that childish experience and to later ones
as well.

* * *

I knew nothing at all about Prague and Bohemia
at that time. For the Slovaks in my part of the
country, there was only one city—Vienna. Folk
went from our parts to Vienna to study and work
and sometimes smartly dressed people came from
Vienna for a visit. Once there came a butcher's
journeyman, in Hungarian costume, with spurs on
his boots and an axe-headed stick in his hand—it
was such a pity he had only one eye, it didn't seem
to go with his splendid get-up. He came to church,
and everybody turned to stare at him because his
boots made such a clatter on the floor. A certain
Viennese Slovak told us travellers' tales about

Vienna: he said there was a bridge there which must be made of india-rubber, because it was so springy when people walked or rode over it. We used to call the Czechs the "dear gentlemen," because they were always saying "my dear!" About Prague I learned for the first time from a children's book called *The Little One's Heritage*; there it described how a certain roving family drove in a cart to Prague, and how beautiful Prague was. I felt myself to be a Slovak. My grandmother in Kopčany always used to bring me white Slovak trousers as a present, but I was dressed like the town boys. When I went to the modern college to study, they had a suit made for me out of my father's old coachman's livery; it was blue with brass buttons—at Hustopeč the boys did laugh at me so!

Hodonín was a great city to me, because it had a church steeple, while at Čejkovice there was only a belfry, the church had no steeple. I knew Hustopeč quite early too; my mother's people lived there. Once I went there to the annual fair; my uncle had given me a whole sixpence, and I bought myself a paint-box; there were cakes of colour and a paint-brush all complete in a wooden box. On the way home a storm came on. The rain came down in torrents; I hugged my paint-box under my arm, under my coat, under my shirt even, to keep it dry. When I got home I had colours all over my shirt and even on my body. So I didn't become a painter that time! Somehow at school I didn't get on with painting; my drawing was better; later on, at the classical college in Brno, I liked geometrical drawing; this was an extra subject, taught us by our mathematics professor. I was a fairly good mathematician; he used to take my part at the staff meeting when I had had disputes with his colleagues.

A Year in a Country Village

When I look back on it all now, what a host of impressions a child has of village life! Winter: there goes St. Nicholas with the Devil. The Devil is a very influential personage; even when I was a professor I still used to play at St. Nicholas with my children. Then you have Christmas, and carol singing; there used to come, God knows from where, a man with a model of the Manger in Bethlehem; it was a show for the whole village. After that there was Three Kings (Twelfth Night), and the masquerades at mid-Lent . . . a child had always something to look forward to. The greatest fun was the quill-stripping; at such times as these as many as twenty people would meet and sit round together—and didn't tongues wag! We children would pinch and nudge each other, so as not to fall asleep and miss any of the ghost-stories; and by and by cakes and tarts would be handed round.

At the first sign of spring we always discarded our shoes; there were still traces of ice here and there, but we would be about bare-footed. As soon as the ground got dry, the high season opened for games with beans or a bat; a ball was a great rarity, especially when it had some india-rubber in its make-up, so that it would bounce back from the ground or the wall; india-rubber was to us a precious commodity, and whenever we could come by a bit of it we cut it up to make a ball.

And then it would be Easter time again, and we would go round with rattles[1] at noon and vespers; on Easter Monday we used to go round and slash at the girls with a willow-switch plaited into a whip, and sing Easter songs for coloured Easter eggs. The Resurrection is a great holiday too; it was the greatest of all at Hodonín, because two dragoons with unsheathed swords used to stand on each side of the sculptured *Entombment*. I simply couldn't take my eyes off them.

Then in May there is the procession and litany in the fields, to pray for good crops; there are the "visitations," when the priests from all the country round meet together with the dean for a banquet— a whole week in advance the cooks were baking and

---

[1] Used at Easter when no bells are rung.—TRANSLATOR'S NOTE.

frying, and we choirboys carried in the dishes. Or there would be a fire in the village, and that too is a holiday for schoolboys; we would be sitting in school, and at the first sound of the bells and trumpets we jumped out through the windows while the girls went rushing out of the doors; in the schoolroom there was a Dutch tiled stove from which we had taken a few of the tiles, and we used to escape out of doors through the gap. Sometimes a boy takes a holiday on his own. My brother Martin was especially addicted to playing truant—we would hunt for him over the whole of Čejkovice. When a boy plays truant he is surprised and quite depressed by the silence everywhere, because all of his playmates are sitting on their benches in school.

Soldiers often rode through the village, and that was always a great event. Another festivity was the raising of the pole[1] at the autumn fair—we boys always tried to climb it afterwards. At this fair the older boys chose leaders, a boy and a girl, and went all through the village from house to house, collecting what they could: fowls, cakes, or wine. . . . Sometimes strolling acrobats would

[1] This is like a maypole except that it figures at the autumn instead of the spring festivities. At this fair the village girls go round slashing at the boys with willow switches as the boys did to them at Easter.—TRANSLATOR's NOTE.

come and stretch a rope across the village green for their tight-rope dancing. Then we boys would imitate them after the fair: we would walk along the top of the garden wall, or the tops of the gables, perhaps even the roof of the church. A fall from there would have been "for ever and ever amen"—only we didn't fall.

A funeral means a holiday in a village, especially if there is music; there is a very festive feeling about this big gathering of fellow-citizens, and more especially "citizenesses," and of course it also provides a welcome chance of leaving one's work and having a good gossip. The parish of Podvorov was joined to ours: when a funeral came from there the bearers used to set down the coffin in front of the cross in the churchyard and go off to the nearest inn to "have a warm up" while the dean or priest was changing his clothes; one of them had to stay outside on the watch for the reverend gentleman to put in his appearance, and then they would gulp down the last drop and shoulder the coffin again. Meantime we choirboys were standing about getting chilly and reckoning how much we were likely to be given in the churchyard—if we were lucky it was a penny; when it was only a ha'penny of course we were most dissatisfied, and relieved our feelings with bitingly sarcastic remarks.

CHILDHOOD

In autumn there were bonfires and grape-picking; then the great jam-making: day and night they stirred the plums over the fire; there was not much talk during the process, but the boys got all the more chances of licking the spoon. Sometimes, at potato-digging time, I had to be out till after dark watching the fields—and I was very frightened of bogies! We did not guard fruit; it was not worth while; it was still green on the trees, and already we'd be after it. To the farmer of those days a fruit tree was a tree and nothing more; fruit was not valued as food—why should it have been?—before the scientists came along with those vitamins of theirs. On the other hand, the vineyards were very carefully watched; the watchman carried a gun; perhaps it was just that which tempted us to go after the grapes. A gang of about twenty of us would get together and see how we could outwit the guard. The campaign was led by boys whose fathers owned vineyards—as they say, stolen fruit tastes sweetest. Of course as soon as I got home they always knew what I had been up to; father would dip his rope-end in water so as to make it sting more! but mother would avert the punishment. But next day the keeper came to the school to complain, and pointed out one boy after another. Excuses were vain; we had to go across the bench, and the teacher or the

39

priest measured us out twenty-five—yes, even the priest!

How beautifully and richly the year is parcelled out in a country village, both by nature and by religion! Life itself is more ceremonial in the country than in the town; it is, as it were, in a setting, even if this setting is made up largely of survivals from paganism. All the customs have the character of institutions; life is regulated by them; they are the accepted order of things. Whoever disturbs the ruling order in any way is shunned by the country-folk. An instance of this was an unwritten law that each family should bake its own bread; that meant getting up at three in the morning to knead the dough which had been prepared overnight—what a lot of work it was! The oven had to be heated and the ashes raked out—then, along with the bread or after it, they baked griddle-cakes of the same dough. How good they used to taste when you spread them with dripping! Any housewife who bought her bread instead of baking it, was viewed with unconcealed scorn by her neighbours. I believe that at my old home in the country almost everybody buys bread now; even in villages the old order is changing. Sunday, again, stresses that ceremonial rhythm of life; I keep the Sabbath even to-day.

After I was grown up I made a deliberate study of country ways; I was spending my holidays at

Klobouky near Brno, and while I was there—I
was a student at Vienna University at the time—I
wanted to write a novel about village life. The local
doctor, an interesting fellow, was to be the hero
and central figure of the novel, and the whole
chronicle of the village was to have been developed
round him. Not long ago I came across a few
pages of that early attempt of mine. Later, when
I was spending my holidays at Bystricka, I observed
year after year the varied way that life goes on in
a village. If our doctors, priests, and teachers cared
and knew how to study these country ways, what
interesting material they would unearth! The
Protestant pastors in Germany have published a
work of this sort; we are still without it; except for
the stories of Božena Němcová. And then, of
course, we have the observations of our younger
novelists. Nowadays all this is passing away; but
our writers still don't seem to be interested—
Heavens, the wealth of still unexplored life there is
in our villages and towns!

On Childhood and Education

The child's first and most important school is
the home; and at home, of course, the real education of a child is not so much what is taught and
preached (in our country there is far too much

preaching everywhere, even at home) as what he sees there. It is the characters of his mother and father, their relations to each other and to the outside world, which have the greatest influence on the child. Think of it: when a child sees disharmony between his parents, quarrels, roughness, lack of respect, untruthfulness, how can he, with such an example before him, unless he overcomes it by his own effort, grow up into a decent fellow? There is a saying: what you pour into the jug will always leave a smell. That is true of families too.

Then you have the relatives, god-parents, neighbours, and their influence—all this in its fullness and concreteness represents the educational influence of the family. The old order—the organized family or clan—has passed away, but its tradition remains in another, freer form, and influences the shaping of the child. The inner circle of relatives are the first people with whom the child comes into contact, and whom he notices—notices sometimes only too well. My favourite among all my relatives was my uncle, a baker at Hustopeč; he was a rough customer, it is true, and used to beat his wife and children, but otherwise he was such a reliable, honest, industrious fellow, a Slovak from Cahnov, a place Germanized in those days. Even in those early days I used to wonder how a Slovak could have become a German; later on when I was at the high school at Hustopeč, I went once during my holidays to visit my relatives at Cahnov and study this change of nationality.

Then a boy gets a chum; they are always about together; they trust each other, they even take each other as model; in the course of years a boy changes his comrades, as though to complete and correct his early choice.

The collections of books and natural objects in a school are a real revelation to the child. Books I used to obtain from Father Satora at Čejkovice; but as for collections of natural objects, we had none. It was not till I went on to the secondary school that I found a small physics laboratory. Then, too, I began to collect insects and pressed flowers. Think what it means to a child if he can get to know his country by means of collections of minerals, plants, and stuffed animals! Of course, such instruction costs money. If only we had enough money for every village to have a satisfactory school with an adequate number of teachers (and in my day I had not so much as heard of women teachers) with, in addition, a varied collection of specimens and books—nowadays every school could have so many of these advantages. . . . If we only had the sense to devote the money to it!

And while we are on the subject of children's books: we call ourselves the nation of Comenius, and yet we have so little children's literature, and still less that is good! I have thought a great deal about the reason for this lack. It is a moral need, as well as an intellectual one. The greater part of our children's literature is mere dull moralizing—our writers make the effort to produce works suitable for children, but they have not the psychological insight to understand the child's mind, to see how truthful and sensible it is in spite of its *naïveté*, or to appreciate its interests and outlook. I am always grieved when, on one of my visits, I am solemnly received by children not in their own words, but in the high-falutin', pretentious words put into their mouths by grown-ups—words a child would never dream of using. It is really clear from our children's books that we do not care enough for our children yet, though we make such a fuss of them.

Well, then, all these influences—home, school, books—affect the development of the child. How many factors contribute to it! To reform education does not merely mean perfecting the teaching in the schools; it means reforming the very lives of adults; we are the soil in which the new generation grows—it largely depends on us whether that generation will be better and happier. That Minister of Saxony was quite right when he told the deputation who came to him with a proposal about the education of children, that children's education was not his business, only the education of grown-ups. And again there is the old question of money. Take education from the point of view of health; the education of defective children, or of the less gifted, the education of neglected children. It is said that a good school saves money which would be spent on prison, hospital, and poorhouse. Proper education and good teaching must be as individual as possible; we are making a series of experiments along those lines in this country, but I would make even more—only of course it needs money to ensure individuality in schools.

Take the social problem in education: children keep the evils of pauperism continually before our eyes. Poverty and want do not mean merely insufficient food and clothing, but those frightful housing conditions. In summer it is all right, but in winter! A whole, large family all on top of each other in one room—think what intimate and often dreadful experiences a child must have in that room. Are not such experiences more profound and fateful than the abstract teaching in school and sermons once a week at church? The social question is above all a question of education.

The question of children's health! I simply cannot understand why, so far, we have never thought enough about playgrounds, swimming pools, and parks for children—the poorer the quarter the more of them there should be, because there are more children. You may even say that with proper watering we could have thick, smooth grass in our playgrounds, as they have in England; and there, again, it is a question of having enough money to do it with, that is the say, of using money for the children—that is the best investment. Of course, there is a difference between town and country; in a village the whole countryside is a playground for the children.

These are problems of upbringing, and side by side with them you have problems of didactics, as, for instance, what to teach; it is well to consider it all deeply. In the first place—religion. Even as a child I thought it ridiculous when in my school report they gave me a mark for "religion." What was it? A mark for the way a boy recited the catechism—but that, after all, is not religion! What we call the religious question is also in a large measure a question of the school, and yet not of the school alone; it is a question for the whole of one's life. We are living in what is undoubtedly a time of transition; we have lived through a profound religious crisis. Scepticism and religious indifference— your real unbeliever is not a sceptic but simply indifferent!—naturally touch the children too. The crisis is really universal, it is in the home also; as

46

a rule you see that the father takes his religion less seriously than the mother—the child gets the impression that religion is a thing for women and children; and so he shakes it off as soon as he begins to grow up. And as long as the school influence lasts, even when the teacher is not actively anti-Church, the child gets many more scientific explanations and impressions than religious ones. And these impressions, this scientific knowledge, consistently thought out, lead the child, while still at school, to religious doubt. In the schools, in the minds of our young people, there is going on in reality the historical process, the so-called conflict of science and faith, the war between science and religion. I lived intensely through all this, though perhaps without suffering any shocks; but for many and many a boy school was a time of most severe crisis. The undenominational school, in countries where the secular school exists, leaves out religion altogether, but I cannot picture a human being in our world growing up without knowing of Christ and His teaching; and of course the Old Testament is part of the fundamental cultural background of every European. Anyone not knowing what Christianity stands for would really be a stranger in our cultural domain; and how could anyone understand European history and the system running through it, if he had not been

47

taught about the reality and development of the Church? But the difficulty is how to teach it, from what standpoint to appraise historical facts—a hard problem for the schools. I myself am always repeating and emphasizing the fact that religion is the essential element of spiritual life and culture, and for that reason not only religious instruction, and instruction about religion in general, but also religious practice is for me a great and unsolved question of school policy.

I see and I am often told that a great advance has been made in artistic instruction in our national schools. It is all to the good if we have pretty spelling books with pictures in them, and good reading books, so that the child shall take with him from school a living need of art. In my time our teacher taught us to play the fiddle, and we used to practise singing, too, chiefly Church music —that was something; to-day they complain of lack of time, there are more subjects to be taught than there used to be, and so they overlook the artistic side of education—well, I think they have only to perfect their teaching methods and there will be more time. In the country where I grew up the whole of education was simpler and more primitive; the country child was not overwhelmed, even to-day he is not overwhelmed, by such a multitude of impressions as a child in the town. But nowadays the country is changing and urbanizing very quickly—not everywhere to the same extent; Slovakia and Ruthenia are even to-day far more countrified than Bohemia—a far-seeing cultural policy must pay careful attention to these differences. Even in my childhood I used to hear it said that the country is healthier than the town, healthier both physically and morally; later on I got to know the unfavourable opinion of the Socialists about towns. My own experience is that a town, even a big city, is not worse morally and has not a worse moral influence on children than the country. Even from the point of view of hygiene the town is not worse, rather the other way—notice the small children in the town and in the country! A town-dweller has relatively better medical treatment and better opportunities for physical culture, especially through sports and Sokol drill.[1] In view of the rapid urbanization of the country, modern education, and

[1] The Sokol movement was a gymnastic organization founded in the last century by Tyrs and Fugner. Its aim was not merely to develop co-operative effort through massed drill, but also to stimulate intellectual activity by means of lectures, libraries, etc., for its members. It was a rallying point for young people with patriotic feelings, and up to and during the war it exercised an important influence on the spirit of the public at large and especially the army, a great number of the Czech soldiers being former Sokols. Since the foundation of the Republic its political aspect is less pronounced, but its history gives it an influence and a standing which no purely gymnastic organization could have.

especially modern physical culture, is just as neces-
say there as in the towns—that is the crucial problem,
and the Government and our ardent pioneers of
social work should bear it well in mind. As for the
question of morality, I should say that immorality
in the country is different from that of the town.
The country is cruder than the town, in its morality
and immorality as in every other way; it is coarser
morally, the town more refined. I should very much
doubt whether the country is, in particular, more
moral sexually than the town. What is written about
that in novels and stories is rather a sign of inaccu-
rate and superficial observation both of town and
country. Moreover, there is a whole specialized
literature on the subject which bears out my opinion.
And there again—another question of education.

And I would say further: parents and teachers
do not merely educate the children; parents and
teachers are also educating themselves through
their children—and that more than one would think.
Through watching a child with love and interest a
grown-up person learns an enormous lot; and if we
taught our children freer, more democratic ways at
school—shall we say in their manners and bearing—we should learn the same thing from them.

As I say, the situation is different now from what
it was in my childhood. Our society has become
more differentiated; beside the farming folk among

whom I grew up, we have industrial labourers and manufacturers, there are many more men with an academic training, there are even more rich people than there used to be. Side by side with the Socialist theories you see the attempt to build up an agrarian philosophy; industry and technique bring with them American ideals; these are very great problems, you know, which also have a bearing on education and the school.

A lot of work is being done now in the field of pedagogical psychology; we have books about the aptitudes of children and young people, about tests and psychometry, about child defectives and delinquents. The study is, of course, only in its infancy, but the fact that attention has been turned to it at all marks a step forward. What we need most is to love our children more, not in words but in deeds, so that we care for them more, and live more intimately with them. This is especially the case with fathers of the patriarchal type. One so often sees a man shovelling together money so that, as he says, his children shall have a better chance than he had; but by the second or third generation the money is all squandered and the family dies out—it is striking how few old and well-to-do families there are in our country. So the best way to care for one's family is to see that the children grow up to be strong, fine, independent individuals.

I so often think about the difference between the country—and of course the town—in my time and to-day! To-day a child is under the influence of the wireless and the gramophone, the newspapers and sometimes perhaps of children's periodicals; to-day people travel much more and with much greater facility—all this kind of thing never existed when we were children. I had nothing to read; I heard of very little; I was not able to travel: that is why the Church was more important than it is to children to-day; it was the only significant building besides the castle; only we could not go into the castle, whereas we used to go to church, and so once a week we saw a building which was larger and airier, which was decorated, where we listened to preaching and music, where we met all the rest of the village—how different the preaching and the whole atmosphere would have to be to-day to attract either children or grown-ups as it did seventy years ago! Here again we are up against the present-day religious crisis and the causes influencing it!

SCHOOLDAYS

SCHOOLDAYS

Apprenticeship

IT was my mother who had me sent to school,
so that, as she said, I should not have to drudge
like my parents. When once, at an inspection of
the school, the Dean himself praised me, they
decided to let me study. My mother was a native
of Hustopeč, so they sent me there to the German
High School; I lived with my aunt, and in exchange
one of my girl cousins came to stay at my home.
I had never thought what I wanted to be; at one
time, when the tailor was making clothes for us at
home, I had thought I should like to do tailoring; I
liked blacksmith's work, that was the trade at which
I had most often seen men working: it is strange,
seeing how religious I was, that I never thought
of being a parson. A boy in an out-of-the-way village
has no living example before him of anything
beyond the circle of farmers and artisans, the
teacher, the chaplain, and dean, the lords of the
estate and their servants, and perhaps a tradesman.
What a boy is to become is not decided so much by
his gifts as by the opportunities that occur.

The High School at Hustopeč was run by a
teaching brotherhood: I remember the Rector, a

stout, handsome, oldish man, and Professor Vasatý.
—he was the brother of the Vasatý in the Young
Czech party—a good-looking young man, proud
of the habit of his order, with its black belt—the
girls used to look on him with favour, too. I was
very fond of this Vasatý: he was the first Czech
from Bohemia whom I got to know, and so he
interested me: he used to chat with me about all
sorts of things. To this day I have a vivid memory
of his way of walking.

I learned easily: I was especially attracted by
physics, that is to say mechanics. I can remember
even now my astonishment when our professor
explained to us that an ordinary wheelbarrow is a
one-armed lever and wheel, and that it corresponds
to that theoretical mechanical formula. That opened
up for me an entirely new outlook on practical
life—I always like to discover theory being worked
out in nature and in society and the home, and to
find a general law exemplified in them: this was a
first revelation to me.

When I had worked through two classes of the
High School I was supposed to go on to the teachers'
training school: but the age of admission there was
sixteen, so the problem arose, what was to be
done with me meantime? I hung about for a while
doing nothing in particular—that was at Hodinín:
my former masters advised my parents to put me

into a trade, so they sent me to Vienna and apprenticed me to a locksmith because I could draw a bit. My master put me at the machine for making the little horse-shoes to go on boots: you put a little rod of iron into the machine, pulled a lever, and the curved horse-shoe fell out. I did it quite well for a day or two; but . . . for a week—two, three weeks . . . at the end of the third I ran away and went back home. I had always liked work, but that monotonous, unvarying work in the factory, just the one or two movements always repeated, was more than I could stand. Perhaps I should have held out, but one of my fellow apprentices stole all my books saved from the High School: always after work I hurried off to read. Having lost them I was so upset that I simply went home to Čejč. I was particularly sorry to lose my atlas: every evening I had travelled the whole world with its aid.

At Čejč my father apprenticed me to the blacksmith on the estate, our neighbour. And how I liked the blacksmith's work! It is work needing strength and speed, over which you must waste no words; you must strike while the iron's hot. At that time there were still castes in the trade: the master was the great authority in the workshop, and after him the journeymen graded according to age or length of service: the journeyman had certain rights, but if an apprentice ventured to do something which he had not yet earned the right to do—to smoke or walk out with a girl—he got a good box on the ear. In summer we often worked in the smithy from three in the morning till ten or eleven at night, mending ploughshares and shoeing horses. But it's fine work: a smith at his forge and at his anvil is master of hard matter. Later on when I was attending a grammar school I once surprised a blacksmith in a village on the way to Brno because I could forge a nail in one heating of the iron. I don't really know whether the fingers of my right hand are crooked from work at the anvil. As long afterwards as the year 1887, when I was at Jasná, Poljaná, Tolstoi looked at my hands and asked me whether I had been a workman.

Perhaps I might have remained in the smithy: but a curious chance befell me there. One day at Čejč I was carrying buckets of water from the well to the forge when a gentleman came along the road and looked at me attentively. I recognized him— he was Professor Ludvík, who had taught me the piano at Hustopeč—but I did not say a word to him: I was ashamed of myself for being so blackened with smoke, and I could see from his expression that he had not expected to find me a blacksmith's apprentice. When I got home my mother said: "Professor Ludvík has been here, and he has left word for you to go to his father, the rector at

Čejkovice, to be his teaching assistant." So that
was how it was decided. I was fourteen years old
and I could not go to the teachers' training school
for two years: so in the meantime I helped in the
school, of course without a salary, only the rector
taught me to play the piano.

Well, I taught the boys and girls as well as I
could, I played the organ in church for some time
every day, I sang at funerals, as school teachers had
to do in those days. And when I recited the Latin
in the funeral service Father Satora used to blame
me for my bad pronunciation. I wanted to understand the words which I had to repeat. It was then,
too, that I had my first conflict with the Church
authorities. I taught the children at school as I
had been taught at the High School, that the sun
is stationary, and that the earth revolves round it.
The children repeated this at home, and their
mothers went to the Dean to complain that I was
contaminating the children and teaching them
unheard-of things, contrary to the Holy Scriptures.
Father Franc managed to smooth them down
somehow. A few days later was the annual fair:
the farmers put their heads together and came to
the school to see me. I was startled: things looked
bad, but I didn't mean to give in. Then one of
them stepped forward and said: "Mr. Teacher,
you're teaching our children all right: just don't

take any notice of our old women, but go on teaching." Then one after another pulled out of his pocket and deposited for me on the piano a four heller piece or at least a two heller piece. . . . It must of course be borne in mind that as a child I too went to the Church school, and that in the country its influence in the 'sixties was still strong.

I loved reading. In the castle at Čejkovice there were some old books left by the Jesuits, books written in the seventeenth and eighteenth centuries, all of them polemics against the Protestants: one of them is rather well known, its title was *Vogel, friss oder stirb*, and it was a bitter refutation of Luther. I devoured these books, and they made me such an ardent Catholic that I converted the wife of the blacksmith for whom I used to work to Catholicism. She was German—her husband had brought her all the way from Germany—and I talked and talked to her until she became converted. It was my first example of a marriage of people with different religions—at that time, of course, I understood it in a strictly Catholic sense. In the German books in the library there were Latin quotations, which I wanted to understand. That was a further reason for learning Latin. I used to memorize lists of words from an old dictionary beginning at A and going through to Z: I had, and still have, a good memory for words. But I didn't make any headway with grammar. After a bit Father Satora gave me regular lessons in Latin.

On his advice I took the entrance examination for the first class of the classical college (gymnasium) at Straznice. So that was how I got to the German gymnasium at Brno in the year 1865.

Brno

Yes, then at Brno . . . I went straight into the second class at the Gymnasium instead of starting at the beginning. I had to provide for myself; my parents could not give me a regular allowance; my mother could only manage—God alone knows how—to scrape a few pence together for me. I lived at first at a shoemaker's in Nová Ulice—there were about six of us there: for two florins a month[1] I had bed, breakfast, and laundry: you can imagine what the breakfast coffee was like! But at least it was hot. Well, I had to raise some money somehow. I gave lessons to the son of a railway official, and that brought me in two florins a month and my dinner on Sundays—I could have eaten three such dinners at once! But they were very nice people; we became great friends. I was top of my class, so I got a recommendation as tutor

[1] One florin (*zlata*) was equal to two Austrian crowns or about 1s. 6d.

to the family of the Chief of Police, Lemonnier;
he was about the biggest man in Brno. Later on I
was given my meals there every day, and so I was
able to keep my brother too, while he was studying.
But he never could get anything into his head. We
boys had a jolly enough time together at our lodging
at the shoemaker's; in the evenings after work we
used to have all sorts of fun: in the summer we went
bathing at Zabrdovice and used to have supper
at the brewery for six kreutzers (1½d.), bread,
cheese, and a pint of beer. What times those were!

I enjoyed Brno because I was able to get books.
Of course at the German Gymnasium I read plenty
of German and Catholic propaganda. But that made
no difference; on the contrary, at that time, just
as formerly at Čejkovice, I simply devoured Catholic
apologetics. I can still remember one or two of the
novels: one was called *Fabiola*, and was by Wiseman.
Fabiola was a beautiful Roman maiden, and she
died a martyr's death. The second novel was also
a translation from the English, and was called, I
believe, *Die Martyrer von Tilbury*: these martyrs
were Catholics, put to death during the English
Reformation. The third book was called *Glaubens-
kraft und Liebesglut* by a certain Mme. Polko: it
was about a young Catholic missionary who went
to India: a beautiful Hindu fell in love with him
there, the Princess Damajanti or something; but his

faith overcame passion, and the story ended again with some kind of martyr's death. I liked all that very much, the missionary ardour, the propaganda of the faith, and especially that constancy in faith and martyrdom: I was quite filled with it.

To be perfectly accurate, what impressed me most in my young days about Catholicism was, first, its living transcendentalism; then the Roman Catholic universality, its international and world-wide scope. And that energetic missionary spirit of propaganda. The effort, too, for a unified outlook on the world and on life. And finally, what is imposing about Catholicism is its Church organization and its authority. Of course as I became a little older I came across anti-Catholic books which exposed the Church's absolutism, her exclusiveness, and acts of violence: even the religious teachers at school drew one's attention to these anti-Church and anti-religious writers by entering into controversy with them. I was growing up at a time of increasing liberalism and its fight against absolute authority, both ecclesiastical and political. Of course I could not even imagine such books as Renan's *Life of Christ* and ideas of that kind. . . .

* * *

In the Gymnasium at Brno our teacher of religion was Father Procházka. He was one of the

Christian Socialists of those days: I went to his meetings and others, and so I got to know about Socialism. When I was in about the fifth form I announced to Father Procházka that I could not go to confession. Father Procházka was fond of me; he was a good and really religious man: he admonished me even with tears, but I would not let myself be persuaded. I disliked all formalism: the boys used to boast of the clever confessions they had made: and besides I was tormented by the everyday practice: to-day my sin is absolved, and to-morrow I shall begin to sin again. "Confess your sin," yes, why not? A man needs to tell everything to a friend, to some kind, understanding person: but don't go and again commit the sin that you confessed. As I say, I did not like its all being so comfortably arranged: and so I stopped going to confession. Of course, doubts about some of the teachings of the Church were already ripening in me.

At that time, too, I had my first conflicts as a Czech. At school we were Czechs and Germans together, and naturally we quarrelled and fought about the comparative excellences of our nations. We Czechs were older, because for one or two years we had had to slog away at German, and I was older by the number of months I had spent at school at Hustopec, and as an apprentice. In our fights—

boyish and quite harmless—we usually beat the Germans. The school was German: but in my days the deputy headmaster was a Czech, a certain Kocourek, author of a Latin dictionary, a good fellow at heart but an object of ridicule to the boys. This Kocourek eked out his salary by making dyes: his hair and whiskers were white, and he used to wipe the dye off his hands on them and then come among us all blue, green, and red. He taught us Czech: it wasn't a compulsory subject, so of course there was always pandemonium during his lessons. Kocourek used to beg us to be quiet, so that at least they should not hear our shouting in the other classes; when nothing else was any good he would offer to tell us a story. Then we were as quiet as mice, and he began. The poor old boy only knew one story, and such a foolish one at that, and he would draw it out as best he could so as to keep us quiet for a long time: but as soon as he came to the point we would break out into such an uproar that he clutched his head and begged us to stop. That's what boys are like!

After Kocourek there came another headmaster, a red-headed Teuton, and with him began a severely German régime. We had a Latin and Greek teacher, who in Kocourek's time still signed himself "Staněk"; but now he began to write it with the German spelling, "Staniek." It made me furious:

and once when he was examining me I scribbled with my pencil in the margin of my book "Staniek = Stanek." He snatched the book out of my hand and, as you may guess, I had a bad time of it. Oh dear! Oh dear!

As a boy I was not conscious of nationalism, or only of a feeling for my own village of Čejkovice. The parish of Podvorov was joined to ours officially, but of course we used to speak of it as "Potvorov"[1] and the Podvorov boys retorted by singing a song satirizing us in the most abusive terms. Every Sunday we used to come to blows with the Podvorov gang as to which should ring the church bells. There you have nationalism in miniature. At Brno I began to understand my Czechdom: before that, at home, I had only felt a primitive kind of socialism. It was through getting to know history that my national consciousness crystallized and my introduction to history was through the novels of Herlos, which I devoured with avidity.

Just consider how exciting our history is: take the Přemyslids, and their whole policy towards Germany: how well they understood our international situation. Then take the Reformation, the counter-Reformation, the national revival—how extraordinarily dramatic is that whole conflict: and

[1] "Potvora" is a term of abuse meaning "monster" or "beast" and -ov is a common place-ending.

then look at the map and our position on it, and consider how we have held out! That, in itself, is a great achievement. Once we thoroughly understand our history we must realize that nowhere in the world can one find a greater one.

We shall always be a small minority in the world, but, when a small nation accomplishes something with its limited means, what it achieves has an immense and exceptional value, like the widow's mite. We are not inferior to any nation in the world, and in some respects we are better, and they are beginning to see this in foreign countries. Our smallness as a nation does not matter; it even has its advantages: we can know each other better, we can live more intimately: we can feel more at home. But it is a great thing when a small nation among great ones does not get left behind, but takes its share in the work of bettering humanity. We too want to ring the bells of the world just as the villagers of Podvorov wanted to ring the bells of Čjekovice. This is the problem of small nations: we must do more than the others, and be very clever; and if anyone tries to get the better of us by force we must not give in. Not to give in, that is the great thing!

*　　　*　　　*

And if we had no Czech books, at least we had folk-songs. We Czech boys at the Gymnasium

67

used to get together and sing songs, each would sing as many as he knew and try to outdo the others; those that we didn't know we learned from each other. I can remember some of them to this day. While I was at Brno I used to go home all the way on foot with some of the other boys from our parts, singing all the way. Once we stopped on the road at a well-known inn, and one of us, the eldest and a gay dog—he became a priest later— began to make up to the hostess, still a young woman and comely. But she was strangely serious. At last, when our comrade took her round the waist, she said nothing, but simply opened the door into the next room where her husband was lying dead on the straw with a lighted candle at his head. . . .

Once I was going back to Brno from home and I had a lot of doughnuts that mother had made for me to add to my meagre fare—perhaps as many as twenty doughnuts. And when I got to the Customs station at Brno the Customs officer stopped me and asked me what I had got there. "Dough- nuts," I said; and he answered that I must pay duty on them. Well, what was to be done? I hadn't any money, and I couldn't bear the thought of parting with the doughnuts. So I sat down by the gate of the level-crossing and we made short work of the doughnuts, my pals and I: yes, and even the strict Customs officer had a taste of them too!

The Wars of the 'Fifties and 'Sixties

Of course as a boy I was keenly interested in war; that was part of one's education in those days. During my childhood and youth there were several wars.

In the year 1859 a fellow came back to our village from the war in Italy: he had got a frost-bitten foot there: I listened breathlessly to the tales of his vicissitudes. He had got the politics of it all very mixed: clearly he did not know with whom he had been fighting or why.

Then in 1863 there was the Polish rebellion against Russia. I was reading the newspapers by then, when I could get hold of them: I was a fierce partisan of the Poles. Several Polish rebels were interned in Olomouc, among them was the Polish woman adjutant Pustowojtowna, and all sorts of legends were current about them in our parts. For some time afterwards I was on the look-out for novels and "shockers" about the Polish rebellion. I had my head full of it all. Later I gave some lessons to a fellow-student who was born in Poland, and he told me a lot more about it: at that time I began to learn Polish.

In 1864 there was the war of Schleswig-Holstein, and I was fanatically in favour of the Danes, because though they were a small country they didn't give in to two big ones.

When the war of 1866 came, we Czech boys at the school in Brno took it into our heads to go as volunteers against the Prussians—that didn't exactly mean that we were pro-Austrian. So we put our heads together and talked it over, and one of our schoolfellows, the eldest and strongest, did really get accepted at once. Then the schools were shut and I went home to Čejč on foot. Soon the Prussians won a victory at Hradec Kralove, and the Austrian soldiers retreated across Moravia to Hungary. Terror reigned everywhere: it was said that the Prussians kidnapped young boys and made them go along with them as soldiers. I got this very much on my mind, so I went to my oldest schoolfellow at Terezova, not far away, and pressed him to come, according to our compact, and volunteer for the Austrian army. Frantík tried to persuade me that it would be better to run away and hide. The Austrian regiments were retreating before the Prussians in the direction of Hungary, and a foraging column marched into Čejc. The Colonel who led them asked which was the way to Hodonín: I offered to guide them. So Frantík and I went with the soldiers. On the way I told the Colonel that I wanted to join the army. He tried to talk me round by all sorts of arguments: that I was young and slight, that no doctor would pass me, that the war was almost at an end, and so on and so forth. When we were coming into Hodonín a house by the roadside caught fire, and that caused a panic: people said that the Prussians had done it, that they had spies everywhere. From Hodonín the soldiers marched on towards Hungary and I went with them as far as Holič: I knew the whole countryside so well and was perfectly at home all over it.

At Holič we were chased by a Prussian outpost and some of the infantry and cavalry turned back to face the Prussians. The fields were full of stacked sheaves and hillocks; the Austrian commander on horseback was behind one of the hillocks. The evening was drawing on and it was getting dark. I hurried with Frantík and a Jew and a Slovak from Holič to a hill near the graveyard, so as to have a view of the battle, and we hid there behind the wall. Frantík was afraid and lay down in a freshly dug grave, the Jew with him. The Slovak and I peeped over the wall; we saw the column of infantry advance and fire—the Slovak said they were Italians and that they would run away. Then the cavalry of both sides charged; we saw how they stabbed and hacked each other. At last a soldier on horseback came riding straight towards us. When he got near

I saw he was the Colonel who had brought me with him, and that he had his face cut open from temple to chin. I called to him, and he rode round the churchyard wall to the gate. The Slovak, who was a sensible fellow, said to me: "Run to the nearest hut, take a sheet from the bed, and wet it at the well." So I ran, and meanwhile he and the Jew (Frantík was still lying in the grave) led the officer after me. I took a sheet from a hut, hung it on a hook, and soaked it in the well: but the wet sheet was heavier than I had expected, and I pulled hard with my knees against the coping of the well so as to drag it out again. While I was doing this I tore the flesh below my knee on a nail, but in the excitement of the moment I didn't notice that. We bathed the officer's wounds and bound him up and took off his clothes—the Jew took them away—and it was only then that I felt that I was hurt. I wanted to run on, but I found I couldn't. I managed to get a lift in one of the army wagons, and at the field dressing station at Pressburg they duly bandaged me up. After that I went with Frantík to Kopčany, where I had relatives. There I heard that the Jew had been taken prisoner by the Prussians, because the Colonel's uniform gave him away, and the wounded Colonel had also been taken prisoner. The fight at Holič, near Stibeničky, was about July 15th, I believe on a Monday; but I do not

72

guarantee the accuracy of the date, and I have forgotten some of the details.

That same year, 1866, I had another adventure. I used to go over to Hovorany to see Father Satora, who had been moved there from Čejkovice. Once I stayed with him till dark: he had an especially splendid funeral to take, and I went along with him. I returned home with one of the funeral candles in my hand. As I walked I saw what looked like a man hiding in a ditch by a poplar tree. I was rather frightened, but I walked on, and as I walked the man jumped across the ditch and caught me by the throat. It was all so quick that I don't know exactly how it happened. I only remember that as he caught me by the throat I hit out at him, he got one foot in the ditch and I hit him across the face with the candle: at the same time he stabbed me in the side with a knife or something. I pulled myself together after that and shot home like an arrow. It was only when I was indoors in the light that we saw that he had cut through my coat and shirt and made a long gash down my side; but it was nothing. I think the man must have been lying in wait for somebody else, and that he mistook me for him.

Later—it was after my first years in Prague— when I began to work on my novel (it was to be a kind of *Dichtung und Wahrheit*) I included that adventure as I remembered it, romatically coloured and touched up (my hero was a soldier, and so on). As you know already I stopped writing that novel long ago and burned the MS.: but even now I sometimes think out bits of it as I lie awake at night.

* * *

Well now, if you must really know, that was not my first attempt at a novel; I began to write my first while I was at the school at Brno. At that time I was already earning my own living, I was supporting my brother while he studied: I was the eldest in my class, I had had battles with the professors, and I had been in love . . . in short, I felt myself to be experienced in all sorts of ways, and so I set to work to write the novel of my life. When I had written several chapters, I read them to my schoolfellows when we went up the river for a day's bathing; of course the boys were keener on bathing and got impatient, but I didn't stop till I had read the whole thing through. Then one of them, a boy from Hana, said: "Tom, such a silly ass story I've never heard in all my life." So I burnt it.

Poetry I had tried even earlier, while I was at Hodonín going through those two classes at the high school: I wrote love poems to a girl there with whom I used to act plays—they must have been horribly formless things, I never had a ghost of an idea of rhythm or form: the boys at school laughed at me for them. It was at that time that I first began to understand what is meant by culture. I should like to have a look at the poems I wrote then. Later at Brno I came across Sušil's *Poetics*, and under his influence I tried making verses in every possible style, including the Indian. . . . Well, later I gave it all up; but literature has attracted me all my life.

* * *

Why did I leave Brno? Well, the reason was really love. While I was in the fifth form my landlady used to have visits from her sister-in-law, a girl of about my own age: and we two fell in love with each other—that was my first great love. I was quite carried away by it; of course I wanted to marry Antonia, and I was always calculating when that would be possible. At that time I was already supporting myself, and I was the eldest and biggest in my class: beside that I had my battles with some of the professors—altogether I felt myself a full-grown and independent individual. Her parents of course forbade her the house; we used to meet secretly, in the street and so on.

The thing was known at school too; and since they could not prevent me in any other way, the director sent for me and spoke, in an offensive way, about my love, as though I had been guilty of some immorality. I was so furious and insulted that I was quite beside myself; when he sent for the school porter to take me away, I snatched up the poker and shouted that I would not stand such insults either to myself or to the girl I loved. That was why I got my *consilium abeundi* for insubordination. They did nothing else about it, because the director himself must have known that he was in the wrong.

Such was my first love: since that time I have meditated a good deal on the subject of love—I was led to do so by my own experiences and by what I observed around me, and chiefly in literature which, of course, is concerned with love to a large extent. I have had a good deal to say about this subject, from my later experiences and under the influence of my wife, but here I will only add this: Love, strong love, real love, the love of man and woman, unspoiled by sex, is, as it says in *The Song of Songs*, as strong as death—it is stronger than death, because it supports life and creates new lives. Literature is right in devoting its greatest attention to love—but on this very subject there is all the difference in the world between what is really literature and what is not.

SCHOOLDAYS

Vienna

Vienna had a decisive importance in my spiritual development: I spent the best part of twelve years there, from 1869 to 1882, during which time I was one year (1876–77) at Leipzig. Moravia was at that time centred on Vienna, and as for Brno it was practically a Viennese suburb. The first time I went there it was as a locksmith's apprentice. Once in the holidays I went there on foot as a schoolboy. Each time I really ran away from the place, it oppressed me so. In my more mature years I grew accustomed to life in the city, especially since it was there that I found the means of educating myself and earning a living.

In the academy in Vienna I was in the sixth form: I matriculated in 1872. I soon found the life at school distasteful, as I was older than the other boys both in years and in experience of life. During my first years in Brno I considered excellence in school work important, and for some terms I was top of my class; but I soon said to myself that it was enough to pass creditably through school and better to supplement one's school work by devoting oneself to languages, art, the reading of historians and philosophers and so on. I was always a voracious reader.

A strong incentive to reading and thinking was

my interest in religion, politics, and nationality. At Brno I had come in touch with the theory of Christian socialism through Father Procházka; I had the opportunity and inducement to think over the problem of nationality as the School itself revealed it to me: pupils and teachers were allotted to classes according to nationality—and as I was made aware of it by the Czech-German environment of Brno, and of course by Czech and Austro-German politics, in so far as I was able to follow them. In Vienna I got into touch with the Czech societies, especially the University students' clubs. As a boy in the gymnasium I was not eligible for membership; so I arranged with the committee that I should register myself as a philosophy student, because for the last two years at the high school until quite recently one took "classes in philosophy." After some time a member of the committee who had ideas of his own about philosophy charged me with having no right to be a member of the club: the boy was right, and so once again I learnt the lesson. A lie has short legs, even when told with the best intentions.

As to my future, I thought very little about it. While I was attending the high school in Vienna I wanted to be a diplomat: I should have liked to go to the School of Oriental Studies, and for that reason I took up a practical course in Arabic; later

78

on, when I saw that the School of Oriental Studies only received the sons of the nobility, I dropped the idea. I think that in contemplating a diplomatic career I let my imagination play too much with the idea of travelling to distant lands. I have always loved to travel, even if it was only on an atlas. I love maps to this day. And I was always interested in the statistics giving the conditions in different places. When I matriculated at the high school my professor of geography set me a question about the statistics of nationality and religion in Hungary: I knew more about it than he did, and that interested him and the inspector so much that they winked at my ignorance of the subjects which didn't interest me.

After matriculating (1872) I went to Vienna University. Of course I had been interested in philosophy for a long time; I remember how I went to Professor Zimmermann and asked him to advise me how to set about the study of philosophy in a business-like way. He suggested that I should read the whole history of philosophy and then choose the philosopher who interested me most as a subject for detailed study.

I had read the history of philosophy and the works of some of the philosophers while I was still at the high school, and had already discovered my predilection for Plato—I have remained a

79

Platonist all my life—so I put down my name for Latin and Greek so as to be able to read my Plato and the other Greek and Latin writers. One of the professors, Vahlen, lectured to us on Catullus for four hours a week during the whole of one term. I had read all Catallus at a sitting, and now this fellow would keep lecturing and lecturing on the number of Catallus manuscripts, the variations in his vocabulary, what a certain other professor had written about him, and what a fool the other professor was. During that time my brother Martin died—he caught a chill in the army and got typhus —and the World Exhibition was opened. The impression made by these events made me dislike philology, though not the Greek and Latin authors.

Then side by side with philosophy I studied natural science (and anatomy too). I was interested in the physiological psychology in vogue at the time. I may say that I did not really want to be a professor. I was not interested in teaching but in learning, and getting to know things myself. As Aristotle puts it at the beginning of his *Metaphysics*: It is in the nature of man to strive after knowledge. Of course it's very fine to get to know something, to be always finding out and learning new things! Lack of interest, indifference, is worse than ignorance.

How does this interest in facts, and then more

facts, fall into line with my Platonism? Why, man, perfectly well. I want to know facts, but I also want to know what they mean and what they reveal. And so now we come to metaphysics.

* * *

How did I manage to live at the University? Well, I used to give lessons; a certain Czech—Bílek was his name—had an educational institute in Vienna; he got me the post of tutor in the family of the banker Schlesinger, director of the Anglo-Austrian Bank; there I finally earned a hundred florins a month, besides my full board, which was more than enough. In the circle of this family and their acquaintances I got to know how the rich live: they are not happy, their wealth isolates them from other people like a wall, and is often the cause of follies and perversities.

For a young man friendship is as strong a feeling as love. I had a dear friend, whose name was Herbert, a fellow-student at the high school, such a frank, nice boy, a lover of history and geography; but he was always in bad health, and at the end of his student days he died. His father had been doctor in the family of some Transylvanian duke or other. I used to go and stay at Herbert's home. His father was dead, but he had a mother and two sisters. I remember him well to this day: my first son was called Herbert after him.

Other friends of mine were my pupil Schlesinger. Všetecka, my colleague at Brno and later professor at Jičín, his friend Weigner, later director of the weaving school at Warnsdorf, and Simon Hájek, later professor in Moravia. Literature made a certain bond between us, but in the main it was sheer comradeship. At Leipzig I made friends with the man who later became the lawyer Dr. Carl Goering. He and I promised each other to try to meet every ten years and tell each other what had been happening in our lives. Well, we never had a formal meeting like that at all, but we have kept in touch.

Herbert inherited a big library from his father, so together he and I read the German classics from the eighteenth to the middle of the nineteenth century; I had already read some French literature alone: Chateaubriand, de Musset, and others. Viennese youth were all reading Hebbel—I have always been sceptical about these fashionable influences. At that time there was a movement among the German students for Wagnerian nationalism, that is, the music and the Germanic philosophy of Richard Wagner and his commentators. I felt no liking for these things, even for the music. Other nationalists at that time were Victor Adler and

Pernerstorfer, who later became Socialist members of Parliament. I had some intercourse with them, but only from a distance. When the second edition of Marx's *Capital* came out—it was, I believe, in the year 1876—I plodded through it conscientiously: his materialistic view of history and his Hegelian philosophy I could not accept at that time. I was greatly interested by the economist Menger, and went to his lectures. Later at Leipzig I attended the lectures of the eclectic Roscher. On the whole I was rather isolated even in my interests.

I never had time to fall into any of the bad habits of youth, because I had to work for my living from the age of fourteen; I did not even go through a crisis at puberty. There is nothing wrong about one's first young love. I have always believed in the purity of youth. The sex problem in youth seems to me altogether artificial and unnaturally stimulated by literature, the theatre, newspapers, etc.

Even when I was at school in Vienna I still went to Hustopeč for my holidays. There I got into touch with the family of the Czech chaplain, and there was a Czech girl staying with them. She interested me because she was the first Czech girl from Bohemia whom I had known. She was gifted and nationally conscious. I entered into correspondence with her, and later it so happened that she came to Vienna. She had a brother who was an official there, and she lived with him. This brother was a curious fellow: he borrowed money from me and seemed, in exchange, to want to let me have his sister. I noticed that he always went out when I came to visit them, and he used to arrange walks and excursions with the same intention. That disgusted me, and I left off going to see them, though I knew that she had no share in it.

I remember another experience: it is, perhaps, typical of youth. I was staying at Klobouky for my holiday, and at a dance there I grew friendly with one of the village girls. I fell in love with her at first sight and wrote to her at once. I calculated how soon we should be able to marry. But no sooner had I sent the letter by the girl who was acting as go-between than I knew that I had committed a cruel piece of folly. And of course the affair came to nothing.

If our upbringing admitted more comradeship between boys and girls there would not be so many of these crises of youth, love tragedies, and disappointments. Just as parents should live in such a way as to set an example to their children, so social life, so-called society, has a serious duty towards young people. When social relations are healthy, then youth is healthy too. I ask you, how is it that these relations are still ugly and slavish for women?

84

SCHOOLDAYS

And while we are on the subject, I will add this. Imagine that even in my time doctors declared that continence was unhealthy for a boy! Once I had a small eruption on my face, and our doctor at home advised me to go to a prostitute, and said that the eruption was a sign of superabundant vitality in the blood. . . . In those days my parents, too, had strange ideas about all sexual matters—of course they were taught them by doctors of that kind. As a private tutor I soon came in contact with the problem of self-abuse among boys. I got to know of this boyish vice at the school at Hustopeč and later at the high school, where some of my pupils had made such a habit of it that they were really ill. I gave some attention to this problem and to the study of sex in general, but that was more especially later when I had become a professor, and was lecturing on ethics and studying social relations and literature. The experts say that the actual harm to health is much exaggerated; that may be so, but in my opinion the moral harm is very great, since it leads to premature and immoderate sex activity, and especially because, I think, it leads to perversion. I have often been given information about the experiences of our teachers of boys and girls—they confirm my opinion. Information about sex should not be insisted on only at school: it is one of the first duties of parents. I remember a beautiful chapter in a novel by Mrs. Canfield, in which she describes a mother explaining the physical side of love to her daughter who has been insulted and upset by the violence of her betrothed. More tact, delicacy, and seriousness in our outlook on these things and in our private life—that is all we need.

Nowadays these things are considered at least a little more reasonably. And sport has done a great deal of good in this respect: to-day a boy who is keen on sport does not smoke or drink or keep late hours, because he does not want to lose his form. If only boys do not become coarsened culturally in the process, then it will be a very great advance and a return to the culture of the ancients, which is what Tyrš wanted. And further, sport has also this advantage, that it supersedes or sublimates innate and inculcated savagery. Every boy is led by nature, surroundings, and history to a one-sided admiration of military heroes and warlike rulers; in sport a boy learns to vanquish his opponent without blood and savagery. It inculcates a sense of honour too. I myself had no opportunities for sport. I only belonged to the Sokols, but even now not a day passes without my doing the Sokol drill.

SCHOOLDAYS

On Schools

The education of boys in our country falls short
on the side of cultivating independence, self-
confidence, and a sense of honour. I was obliged
to be independent as a child because I had to earn
my bread far from my home, and I looked after
myself altogether and decided everything for myself;
so my case is different. But our whole educational
system leads to anything but a plucky outlook on
life. The mere desire for material security, prefer-
ably in a Government post so as to be sure of a
pension. . . . I see fear in all this, fear of a life
of enterprise, of responsibility, of mastery. It is true
that we lack a sea-coast, we lack the consciousness
that there is another world on the other side of it;
we sit like frogs in a pond croaking to one another.
I am always glad to hear of one of our people going
out into the world and succeeding there; not as
emigrants—emigration is a form of flight—but as
enterprising Czech conquerors. Of course, poverty
has much to do with it. The majority of our people
are only one or two generations removed from
humble folk, farmers, peasants, and craftsmen. A
boy coming from such a home is on the look out,
not for what he would like to do, but for a "job"
at which he can get his living comfortably. Even their
"culture" is only a superior kind of trade, and

perhaps they wouldn't even succeed in a regular trade.

I have noticed that the best teachers—especially in the middle schools—are the specialists. When a professor is really keen on his subject, he awakens a love of it in his pupils. Of course one forgets almost everything one learns at school, but interest once awakened lasts and enables one to notice things. Knowledge without interest is dead. The business of the schools is not so much to teach a great number of facts, but first to give the pupils habits of accuracy, attention, and method: to teach them how to observe nature and life for themselves, and make them able to solve its various problems, great or small, when and wherever they arise.

Yet when a professor does happen to want to teach like that, then he preaches. In our country they preach not only in church, but even in school, in the newspapers, and in Parliament. Of course the science of developing youth is an extremely difficult thing—the middle schools for the most part only cultivate didactics: they impart knowledge far more than they educate. A boy at the middle school comes under influences which his professor either does not suspect or else overlooks. In England, for example, a schoolboy has much less superficial learning than in our country, but on the other hand the English school forms character. In our schools

88

a small boy must get hold at least temporarily of a whole host of subjects, whether they interest him or no: but to mix with people, to get on with them, to react to the real influences of life—that he is not taught. Our schools too often turn out clumsy, slow-witted, "green" youths: the cleverer and more energetic stultify in rebellion—the school may be said to be poison for them and the teacher a tyrant. Yes, even I used repeatedly to have the nightmare that I was going in for my examination again. The secondary school should not be a place of punishment, and one should not have to look back on it as a nightmare. When school is a burden, the weak only learn in fear and the strong in rebellion; both heave a sigh of relief when they get through those seven or eight years, during which they were growing up physically and spiritually—seven or eight such important years! That is slowly changing too: the old middle school was too much a place for turning out future officials, genuine Austrian bureaucrats. Now it has and will have a different duty. But I want to say this: if we are to talk of a "crisis of intelligence," we must get down to the roots of it, and that means reform the schools.

I grew up rather isolated—at school in Brno I was older than my schoolfellows and thrown back upon myself: in Vienna my surroundings were strange, and I was already twenty years old, while my fellow-students were still children. Perhaps that is why I took up a sceptical and critical attitude to the movements of the times. But among our young people it is easy to see how youth flings itself from one extreme to the other—every five years there is a new generation which throws aside all that has gone before. One reason is that we are a small nation, and have been cut off for centuries from the great world of culture, so that we are always trying to get even with it. That is why we seize on each new thought—sometimes from the East, sometimes from the West, sometimes from we don't know where; that is why our cultural development is so disconnected. It is good to take a look at what is over yonder, but it must be a look embracing the whole horizon, and we must have a try at all the different things there are. Let us say that we must open our windows to foreign influences; very good, but then we must open all our windows, and all our doors too! Of course a small nation, and especially ours, which was thwarted and cramped in its development, is thrown back on the culture of the greater nations. But we have plenty of examples of small nations which have been prominent culturally and have given a great deal to humanity; in this respect historians and politicians are still far too much influenced by the opinions of the outside world on what constitutes a nation's worth. Hence the misunderstanding all over Europe, which is made up of a number of small nations.

And another mistake we make is in underestimating what we are and what our country has. There are people who are always sighing that America is larger than we and Paris livelier than Prague. Because of what we have seen abroad we can't see what we have at home. I know that one cannot, for example, appease one's intellectual curiosity merely by reading Czech literature; but one must know it through and through to understand all that it signifies. The man who merely scoffs at us for living in a small way is scoffing at himself too; it is his own fault that he lives so pettily. This is especially true of young people. Your *parvenu* gentleman does not want to live in a small town or in the country, because, he says, he is culturally buried and stunted there. In reality it is a question of comfort: he can only be culturally alive when he has the artistic stimulus of his café associates. As a proof, think of the poet Březina! Wisdom and culture are things of the spirit, not a matter of chance surroundings. A lion is a lion even in a cage, he doesn't turn into a donkey.

It is among our young people that I am most aware of our lack of tradition. Of course we are far too prone to follow the beaten track; we do not realize the extent to which we do it; but to run along rails already laid is not yet tradition: tradition is the common work of the generation, a common and public discipline. We in our country often begin from first principles instead of getting into touch with the work of our predecessors; that is why we have so many programmes and so many small groups like sheep-pens, which can exercise comparatively little influence on real life and development. In truth we are a young nation and, moreover, we are a society which is always being renewed from below. The Counter-Reformation deliberately wiped out the tradition of the Reformation—there you have a gap of three hundred years —and to-day we do not know how to profit by either the one period or the other, nor by the one which preceded them. For me the chief cause of our lack of tradition lies in this religious indifference: that is why our average intellectual has no use for our past, in which religion played such an important part. Instead of some great tradition of this sort our intellectual has his circle of friends at the café, or round the table at the tavern, or some local or technical organization of his political party. It is this stuffy atmosphere of club-rooms which really constitutes pettiness in life.

Nowhere in the world do you hear folk grumble and complain as they do in our country: it is the lack of the plucky outlook on life, and something worse besides. I think that everyone who is discontented in this way must dislike his profession: that is why he inveighs against politics, conditions, and the whole world. The man who does his job without interest, and only to earn his bread, is an unhappy and vitiated individual. I love to listen to a man talking with affection and keenness about his work: what a lot you can learn by listening to him! Have you ever seen Esperanza Garrigue (the teacher of singing[1]) listening to a young singer: did you notice how her eyes lit up? I was immensely attracted by the way she threw herself into whatever she was doing. It is a thing to which parents and teachers should pay attention, and find out from what their young people derive inspiration. We have schools of all sorts, practical, agricultural, and technical, so that each can choose according to his ability and inclination. In a democracy there is no need to be always planning from childhood for a boy to become a "gentleman"—in reality some quill-driver in an office. A farmer, a craftsman, a workman is often a better man than your intellectual: only let each one be a man, each man in his right place, each a complete individual.

And girls? It is exactly the same for them.

---

[1] Sister of Charlotte Garrigue. See p. 116.

THE YOUNG MAN

THE YOUNG MAN

The Reader's World

MRS. BROWNING says in *Aurora Leigh* that a poet can have two nationalities. I don't know about that. But it is often said that to know an extra language means to live an extra life. As to that I have a certain amount of experience.

German I got to know as a small child, from my mother; but German was never a second mother-tongue to me—of that I was well aware when I went to the German school at Hustopeč. The boys used to laugh at my German, and I had some difficulties with the lessons given in German which were only surmounted when I went to the high school, and even then did not vanish altogether. When I published my *Suicide* a well-known German writer read it with particular attention to the style: he found about a dozen Slavisms in the book. In German surroundings I talked Czech almost continuously, at my rooms, with my friends, in Czech circles; I heard German at school, and German was the language in which I gave my lessons; moreover the bulk of my reading was in German.

I soon got as far as Goethe and Lessing. Goethe at first charmed me more by his lyrics than by

Faust; through Lessing I discovered the fascina-
tion of the Greek and Latin writers. Besides which
German opened up a world of literature to me,
especially in its translations. Shakespeare and the
other great ones I got to know first through German.

Under the influence of Vienna I read a good
deal of Austrian literature, Grillparzer and others;
I endeavoured by means of that literature to get to
understand Austria and Vienna. I was especially
interested in writers from Bohemia (Hartmann and
Meissner), and I still read our writers of German
with the same attention. Of those born in Hungary,
Lenau especially charmed me both by his poetry
and his life; K. Beck was also a Hungarian. I met
him in Vienna.

French I began to teach myself at Čejkovice,
while I was teaching there. Satora proposed to me
and the junior teacher that we should learn French;
he taught us himself, for although he did not speak
the language, he knew the grammar very well, and
Latin helped him. But the lessons did not last long.
I began studying French by myself when I was
in the third class at school; it interested me to
compare French grammar with Latin. At that time
I was teaching a fellow-student at his home, where
there was a French girl, also giving lessons. So I
took pains to pick up the pronunciation. It is said
that people with a musical ear get hold of a foreign

98

pronunciation better—that would be a good thing
for us Czechs and Slovaks, if we are, as we insist,
so musical. I read French wherever I came across
it. Though I had very little money I bought myself
French text books on history, geology, and so forth.
I read novels: Balzac, Sand, Dumas, Hugo, but
Renan interested me more, and Père Hyacinthe
influenced me too, in those days. It was only in
Vienna, at the University and later, when and
wherever I had access to libraries, that I began
to study French literature systematically—I got
hold of Rabelais of course—it was in him that I
felt the real French character. Molière attracted
me very much. Among the poets my favourite was
de Musset; as for Chateaubriand, I translated
some things of his myself; he was so akin to my
romanticism. Of thinkers I liked Descartes, and
later Comte; I was deeply interested in Pascal. In
De Maistre I studied Catholicism. Rousseau held
me as much by his *Héloïse* as by his *Contrat Social*.
I read Voltaire but he did not make any special
impression on me.

The French spirit is an admirable thing. It is
said that the French characteristics are "logic and
clarity." That may be so; I should call it "deduction
and consistency." At the same time they possess
that strong spirit of enterprise. The French Revolution and French socialism gave the world new

99

problems and new solutions, French art, French literature evolve more and more new ideas. Add then the French feeling for form—really we have in the French the true successors of the Romans, and a living fount of classical culture.

Paradoxical as it may seem, it was because I read French literature so much and so continuously that I never wanted to go to France. I think that was a mistake, one understands better when one takes in a nation through one's eyes as well. But I had not enough money for it, and when at last I went abroad, I chose a country which I did not know so well through its literature. I still follow French literature as far as my time allows me.

From the beginning I welcomed French as a counter-weight to German influence. I was grieved that so many of our people were only superficially enthusiastic about France or Russia (when, for instance, they sang "Russia is with us! Who is against us, him the French will smite!"), while in practice their knowledge of foreign languages was restricted to German. I took our Francophilism and Russophilism concretely, and tried to get an understanding of their literature and their spirit. And so, if you please, I have sometimes been called a Germanophile! I, who more than most Czechs, was brought up on non-German literatures, especially, as I say, on French and Russian. How I studied the latter my book on Russia bears witness. Certainly I had no sympathy with those Slav enthusiasts of ours who did not even learn the Russian alphabet. Among the Russians my favourites were Pushkin, Gogol, Goncharov, and Gorki. Tolstoi I admired as a great artist, even when I disagreed with his opinions. Dostoyevsky attracted me in a negative way; I could not accept those Russian and Slav anarchist strains in his character which, in spite of his return to orthodoxy, he never overcame. Through his duality he became the father of Russian Jesuitism. In Turgenyev there is something that I dislike. The other Slav languages I can read more or less, but I prefer translations: Mickiewicz and Krasinski attracted me very much.

English and American literature I came to know later, chiefly through the influence of my wife, and I know them pretty thoroughly through many years of reading. I read them to-day more than ever, and consider that their novels are, in both form and content, more interesting than those of other literatures: one learns more from them, and they reveal many fine and wise experiences.

Italian I can read and, if necessary, even talk; but most of the Italian authors I read in translations (French, German, and English); of their philosophers I especially like Vico. The literature of the other nations I know only in translation.

Yes, from my childhood to this day I have been an insatiable reader. I have written studies of my attitude to literature; perhaps I may publish them. In them I have tried to depict the influence of a foreign nation, to what extent we are able to acquire its language, how far we can enter into and assimilate its spirit, and how much our own characters are influenced intellectually and morally by our contact with it. For quite a long time I planned to set down my opinions in a study like *The Diary of a Reader*, containing all one reads from one's eighth or tenth year upwards. What quantities one reads!

I have read, far longer than I can remember, the great poets side by side with the philosophers, and perhaps more than they: and of what are called "the poet thinkers" Goethe interested me no less than Kant—more, even—and so did the other poets from Shakespeare downwards. Dante somehow remained inaccessible to me. Poets and all artists meditate on life and its problems no less than philosophers, and at the same time their thought is more concrete; to those who can read them they give an extraordinary wealth of knowledge; and if we want to know the soul and spirit of foreign nations, art is our surest way to that knowledge.

Unless I know the language I do not feel at home in a foreign country, I do not see into it. That is why I deliberately only travelled to coun-

tries where I could talk with the people in their
own language. Well, yes, of course, I went to
Egypt, Palestine, and Greece, but I went there for
the sake of their ancient culture, not of their present-
day life.

I am consciously European in my culture—by
that I mean that European and American culture
(America is ethnically and culturally a fragment
of Europe, transported—though not completely—to
America) satisfies me spiritually. Eastern philosophy
and literature I know very slightly and only at
second hand, because I do not know the Oriental
languages. The culture of India, China, and Japan
is inaccessible to me. I am very sceptical of those
opinions which exalt them above European culture;
they could, of course, retort that I am speaking here
like a blind man about colours.

And as a European I am a Westerner—I say
this for the benefit of those Slavophiles who see in
Russia and Slavdom something super-European.
The best Russians were Westerners too!

I feel in our young writers a powerful artistic
force and an urge towards that which is world-wide,
towards a world standard. Until the war and
immediately after it our spiritual strength was all
concentrated in one direction, on politics; and the
general poverty also told against us. A Czech writer
could not live by his pen. Our independence, our

Republic, must liberate our spiritual life: that will benefit and actually bring prosperity to our literature, as we see by the interest abroad in our literature and in our art as a whole.

All my life I have tried to enter into the thought and through it the culture not only of our own and other Slav literatures, but of Greece, Rome, Germany, France, England, America, Italy, Scandinavia, and Spain, though less in the case of these last. I have tried to make an organic and appraising synthesis, and I think that I have brought all these influences into harmony with our national standpoint. But the decisive influence which formed my opinion was not, I believe, that of the poets and philosophers, but of life, my own life, and the life of our nation.

The Student

In my student years in Vienna the person who had the greatest influence on me as a teacher and man was the philosopher Franz Brentano. I used to go and see him at his house very often—his lectures (which were in the afternoon) I could not attend since I was tied to my duties as tutor. Franz Brentano had been a Catholic priest, but he left the Church because he did not agree with the Vatican Council and the doctrine of infallibility. That

Council was a stumbling-block for me too. But Brentano never spoke of religious problems either in his lectures or in conversation; the only step he took was to leave the Church. He helped me immensely by his emphasis on method, empiricism, and perhaps most of all by the example of his profound criticism of the philosophers and their teaching. Kant was his favourite target. Brentano had a very great influence on thoughtful students.

There were other philosophers whom I knew personally at Leipzig, in particular Wundt. I attended their lectures and came into contact with some of them in philosophical circles where there was lively discussion. I myself lectured at one of these, on present-day suicide. I concentrated more on theological lectures than on philosophical, attending those of Luthardt, Fricke, and others. What Leipzig did for me above all was to help me to understand Protestantism.

But the philosopher who influenced me most strongly was Plato. Primarily through his interest in religion, ethics, and politics and his extraordinary combination of theory and practice. In Plato, too, there is that beautiful and astonishing synthesis of world opinions, even though it springs from certain imperfections, that is to say from the fact that the degree of development of those days set no precise limit to the various branches of science. Another thing which deeply attracted me to Plato was that he was a great poet and artist. I have always loved poets, and read them as much as the philosophers, perhaps even more.

Yes, to this day I am a Platonist: I could prove it to you from my relation to the theory of evolution. Don't be afraid that I shall begin speculating on Darwinism, neo-Darwinism, Lamarckism, vitalism, and so forth. I accept Plato's idea in this form: I believe in the idea of life, by which I understand that life is one but is incarnate in a multitude of forms; each creature is, as a creature, like all the others in something because, like them, it is alive. And yet each differs from all the others. By means of their similarity I can build up from that multitude of creatures the whole scale of created things from the simplest form to man. This gradation, this hierarchy, we encounter in every sphere whenever we compare, arrange, appraise. If you ask how these diverse forms and species originate, I answer that I do not know: but I do not accept Darwin's theory of mechanical evolution, I do not accept his principle of selection in the struggle for life. For all his English empiricism, Darwin has a fantastic method in the very fact that from the methodical scale according to likeness he made a descending scale of evolution. In opposition to Darwin the natural scientists placed Lamarck: neo-

Lamarckism makes a concession to Darwinism, neo-Darwinism makes concessions to Lamarckism in various respects. Finally the vitalists, also of various schools, give tongue. As a layman I gather from all this the information that as yet we know nothing scientifically about the real origin of species, and especially of new species. To my mind Darwinism is one of the forms of historicism and relativism against which I have always defended realism. I do not believe with Haeckel that the majority of creatures developed from a few original species or from one original species, and I do not believe, as I say, in the differentiation of species by mechanical evolution.

I maintain the hypothesis of a Creator; in a Creator my ideas have a certain metaphysical basis, since belief in a Creator has always existed in some form or other. As you see, we can't do without a little metaphysics: but I hope I have not gone beyond the reserve which I impose on myself in these matters.

From Plato I naturally came to Socrates; and it goes without saying that I compared him with Jesus—Jesus was to me religious progress, Socrates the philosophical apostle. That irony of his! He stops the high priest in the street and questions him for a long time about religion, until the Greek priest himself must admit that he is a blockhead.

Or he talks to a general about the army, or a sophist about sophistry, and shows how these people do not really think intelligently even about their own job. Just think what times those were: an educator like Socrates, a philosopher like Plato, a scholastic and systematist like Aristotle! Think what Aristotle meant to the Middle Ages and to humanity! His relation to Plato is peculiar; he was Plato's pupil, he listened to his teaching for twenty years, he is a Platonist, but he is more mature because in him the Platonic addiction to myths is moderated. Platonists and Aristotelians are, in fact, two types: I became aware of this in my relations with Brentano, who was altogether the Aristotelian type.

When I was in Athens not long ago what surprised me most was to find that there are neither steps nor a regular path leading to those temples on the Acropolis: they set the temple in the midst of nature, as if it grew there of itself out of the soil. It was the Romans, those greater formalists, who first built steps to their temples. In just the same way Greek philosophy, science, poetry, and art spring up in the midst of nature and the primitive life of Greece—a revelation, as the Old and New Testaments are a revelation of the desert of Palestine and of primitive Judaism.

Since we are speaking of the ancients and the Jews, think of this: these two small nations, the

Greeks and the Jews, had and have still an influence on the whole of cultured humanity. The Greeks gave us art, philosophy, science, politics; the Jews theology and religion. Before them there were Egyptians, there were Babylonians, but their cultures were really assimilated and perfected by the Greeks. The whole of Europe is still living on antiquity and Judaism: we hardly know it, but antiquity is in everything. It is clear that American culture, on the other hand, did not grow straight out of classical culture. There is a new element in it, a pioneer element, a practical optimism; for that reason we have something to learn from them just as they have from us. We are the inheritors of the Middle Ages too; Catholicism absorbed much of classical culture and adapted it to its own ends. This was in its way an advance. There are classical elements even in the Scriptures. For that reason some of the Church writers should be included among the authors read at school.

We in our northern climate possess something which the ancients, for all their culture, had not got: that warm relationship to home and hearth and family, to wife and children. The Greeks and Romans lacked our winter; they did not know what it means to sit by the warm fireside with the children gathered round mother and grandmother. They talked politics and philosophy in the street;

we shut ourselves up indoors and speculate over books. Finally your Russian sits behind the oven and doesn't even think, he just muses. The farther north, the more isolation and seclusion, and the more family life. Look around you and see how the trees are turning gold and changing colour! Each season of the year gives us a different beauty, different impressions, and the more complex and intensive farming befitting the climate. The Italians have not got this, and you do not find it in the ancient writers.

* * *

Of course I am in favour of classical education: only it must not be mere juggling with words. It is always good to get to know the spirit of another nation. Greece and Rome were comparatively primitive in their religion, science, philosophy, and art, as well as in the technical, economic, and political sphere: it is easier to get to the kernel of things. And this primitiveness is somehow congenial to young people. The clearness and logic of the classical languages has something to do with it: Latin and Greek grammar inculcate accuracy and punctiliousness in thought and word. And the great beauty, purity, and harmony in their art! Beauty of form and artistic perfection are eternal. Homer, Sophocles, Aeschylus should be read in school, and in maturer years Euripides; and extracts at least from Theocritus. In Latin, Vergil, Horace, Tibullus, Propertius, and of course the historians; one or two speeches from Cicero are enough: his philosophical effusions are chiefly interesting to students of the Greek philosophers who can judge how much Cicero pilfered from them. The Greek language was to the Romans what Latin was in the Middle Ages and French was later—*vox exemplaria graeca nocturna versate manu versate diurna*! I remember that line—the Romans too were faced by the problem of bilingualism, and were not ashamed to learn a foreign language. Greek was no obstacle to the Legions in their conquest of the world! But if we're reading the Latin authors at all, then let's be thorough about it: why not read St. Augustine at school, and perhaps a bit of Plotinus? I think they should be read in the original, but with a good translation to hand. We have a few fine translations now; if I had the money I would start a fund for publishing standard translations of all the classics. Wait a minute—how much would that cost? It would be an excellent thing. After that I would publish translations of the standard writers of other nations. And good biographies, we need them too. Besides that I would found a museum of sculpture. And I have a plan for a standard library of living authors, the library of the educated man; I lie and think over it when I can't sleep. Just think what splendid work we have before us! Some day, perhaps, we shall pluck up courage to follow a real cultural policy.

Other philosophers who influenced me? In particular Comte, Hume, and Mill. And it must not be forgotten that we are also influenced by persons and writers with whom we disagree.

* * *

Czech life in Vienna centred round the workmen's clubs, the Beseda,[1] and the University students' club. The greater part of the members were Moravians: there were a few from Prague, whom I liked less. For three terms I was President of the University Club. You ask why? Well, someone had to be president, and I had a little money. I left it nearly all in that club: there were so often things it needed. It never once entered into my head to save my money.

At that time we arranged a celebration in honour of Alois Vojtěch Šembera—yes, the man who wrote the history of Czech literature: he was reader of Czech at Vienna University. He took part in the

[1] The Czech society formed in every foreign city where Czechs are living.—TRANSLATOR'S NOTE.

battle of the Manuscripts[1] too; he was against them, and was so bitterly attacked for it that his only son, a most gifted man, became a renegade: he deliberately turned German. Besides this son, Šembera had a daughter, Zdenka, a good deal older than I; she was very gifted and energetic, and was a splendid example to the students of what an emancipated woman can be. She helped us to organize the celebration in honour of her father. After I left Vienna I used to write to her from Leipzig.

My first printed work in Czech was an article on "The Patriotism of Plato." It appeared in a Moravian year book, which also published my next essay, one on "Progress." I was writing then under the *nom de plume* Vlastimil (meaning "lover of his country"). In my later conflicts in Prague my chauvinistic opponents reproached me with having dropped the name when I entered the German University; as a matter of fact I dropped it because I was ashamed to broadcast my deepest feelings of patriotism in such a way. All the same, while I was lecturer at Vienna University I published my Czech lecture on hypnotism. I wrote political reflections on

[1] Some clever forgeries purporting to be Czech literary works of an early date, and claimed by Czech nationalists as proofs of their nation's great literary past. Masaryk was one of those chiefly responsible for showing up the forgeries, and was regarded by fanatical nationalists as a traitor to his people.—TRANSLATOR'S NOTE.

activist policy in the paper *Moravska Orlice* ("The She Eagle," emblem of Moravia), and I sent Vaclav Vlček some articles for his *Osveta*. He did not publish them, I think because my Czech was very rough and bristling with Russianisms—I was deep in Russian literature at the time.

My doctor's thesis (1876) was on *Plato on Immortality*. I burnt it later, together with many other manuscripts. There was a certain amount of good in it, but not enough, to my mind, to justify keeping it.

I was already Doctor of Philosophy when I went to Leipzig in the autumn of 1876. Leipzig means to me the place where I met my wife.

At the University I was working in philosophy and theology. I studied Protestantism, and the form it took in the various lands which adopted it. An expert can see from that what my development was in the religious question, and how I ripened. For the time my ideas were not clear or decided enough.

I used to go to the Czech Club: the members were chiefly workmen, but I got to know a Lusatian[1] writer there, called Pjech (spelled Pech in German), an ardent lover of Havlíček. I had been interested in Havlíček since my schooldays: we used to copy

---

[1] The Lusatian Serbs, small numbers of whom are still found scattered about the Elbe basin, are the remnants of the original Slav inhabitants of Saxony and Prussia.—TRANSLATOR'S NOTE.

his satires, and anyone else's we could lay our hands on, in those middle 'sixties.[1] Pjech insisted to me that the Czechs ought to study Havlíček more seriously than heretofore. Owing to a curious development, I was able to respond to his appeal.

I was interested, too, in studying and observing the Lusatian Serbs. Dresden was a centre towards which they drifted, and now and then I managed to chat with them as they crowded round the Catholic Chapel Royal. I specially noticed in Pjech, who was the translator of Pypin-Spasowicz into German, the process of Germanization of the Lusatians, and yet for all that how Slav they still remained. Later I used to go from Prague to Budyšín (in Saxony) and continue my observations.

During that time in Leipzig I became interested in spiritualism. I had already read a good deal about different kinds of occultism in Vienna: in Leipzig I came among spiritualists, and was able to observe them. This interest led me later to a careful study of hypnotism. But I need hardly say that I was not impressed by spiritualism and occult apparitions:

[1] Havlíček (1821–56) was one of the little band of Czech patriots who started the national revival in the 1840's of last century. He was a clever journalist and a biting satirist, clear-sighted and honest, and never afraid to face truth and reality. Unlike some of his fellow workers, he looked to the present and future rather than the past: he believed that the past was valuable only in so far as it strengthened and inspired present and future action.

there are some apparitions that we do not understand
—but what, after all, do we understand?

Miss Garrigue

At Leipzig in the summer of 1877, a fateful
event took place which proved decisive for my whole
life and spiritual development: my meeting with
Charlotte Garrigue.

I had heard a lot about her and her family,
especially her father's family, from Mrs. Goering,
who kept the *pension* in which I stayed at Leipzig.
The Garrigues, so I heard, were descended from
an old Huguenot family which fled to Holland and
finally settled in Denmark. Mr. Garrigue was born
in Copenhagen, and became a great friend of Thor-
waldsen the sculptor. He got to know the Goerings
when he was at Leipzig in a publishing house. Then
he emigrated to America. His wife, Charlotte's
mother—who was a Miss Whiting—was from the
west of America, and also of an old Puritan family.
A father descended from Huguenots, a mother from
those pioneers in Western America—what a tradition of vital and moral energy!

In the year 1870 Mr. Garrigue visited Germany
with part of his family: Charlotte was already devoting
herself to the study of music, especially to the piano.
She had the opportunity of visiting Liszt, and she

116

heard much of him and his musical circle. She used to go to concerts at the Gewandhaus and to hear motets at St. Thomas' Church, where they still preserved the tradition of Bach, their one-time choirmaster. Her greatest friend at this time was the pianist, Maloruska Kirpotina. In 1877 Mr. Garrigue sent her back from America to the Goerings to study at the Leipzig Conservatoire, though a partial paralysis of the hand interfered with her musical career.

Naturally I was curious about her even before we met. When the time came for her to arrive, I waited by the window to see her alight from the carriage. One day we all went for an excursion near Leipzig to the former Slovak village which impressed Kollar so much. While we were being ferried across the river, the boat ran against the shore, and Mrs. Goering fell into the water. The poor woman was terribly stout, and would have been drowned: so I jumped after her and pulled her out. I must have got a chill from my wetting, and the doctor ordered me a few days at home. This prevented my going to lectures, so I suggested to Miss Garrigue and Miss Goering that we should do some reading together. We read English books, some poetry, and chiefly John Stuart Mill's *Subjection of Women.* We began to get near to each other then.

Charlotte went away to Elgersburg near Thuringen to stay with her friend. When she was gone I realized what my feeling for her was, and I wrote to her proposing marriage. Her answer was uncertain. So I plucked up my courage and went after her—I could only afford fourth class on the train—and we fixed things up between us.

Then Charlie went to America and I went back to Vienna. I plunged into my work on *Suicide* for the thesis to qualify me for a post at the University. Suddenly I got a telegram from Mr. Garrigue saying that Charlotte had had a fall from the carriage and was badly hurt, and that I was to come at once. When I was all ready for the journey there came a letter from her saying that it wasn't so bad as all that, and that I was not to interrupt my work. But I was anxious, and I went all the same, in 1878, in the ship *Herder*, via Hamburg and Havre, to America. In those days the voyage took twelve or fourteen days: but our passage was exceptionally stormy and we took seventeen days. The *Herder*, like all the ships of the Hamburg-America line, was very bad. She went down on her next voyage, and the *Schiller* was lost in the same way. Once during the night, when I was lying in my bunk, there was an awful noise and water came dashing against the cabin door: I thought that we were going to be drowned. It was very curious: all the other passengers became panicky and rushed about shrieking and praying. But I lay quite still and waited to see what would happen. . . . And it was only a cask of drinking water after all that had got smashed! When I arrived I found Charlotte nearly well again.

But what now? I racked my brains what to do: whether to stay in America and find employment there, for I had lost the lessons which supported me in Vienna by going away. I might perhaps find a post in America at a University or on a newspaper; however, we decided that I should go back and finish the work for my thesis. I asked Mr. Garrigue to give us the money to live on for three years until I could support a family. Mr. Garrigue was an old viking and American, and in America it is taken for granted that when a man marries he can support his wife himself. So he refused at first to give us anything resembling a dowry for his daughter. Finally he gave us three thousand marks (£150) and our passage back to Vienna, and for some time afterwards he used to send us money now and then. Our wedding was on March 15th, the civil marriage at the Town Hall in the morning and the religious ceremony in the evening at home in the family circle. A week later we were on our way to Vienna. It was on this journey that I had my second look at Prague.

* * *

I think I have already mentioned that Charlotte's family was Danish on the father's side; her mother was American, and both families can trace their descent back several centuries. The Garrigues came from the South of France—there is a range of mountains there still called La Garrigue—and they are supposed to be descended from the Capets and ultimately from Louis IX, St. Louis. On the mother's side, too, the family is old—I might almost say aristocratic. Her ancestors were among the Pilgrim Fathers. On my side my children have Slovak peasant blood and more of it: perhaps it is not less ancient, and a fine peasant or workman ancestor is no less worthy. Yes, it was nice that Charlie brought the tradition of gracious everyday manners and the feeling for freedom and honour. A strange thing is that the painter, Schwaiger, who associated a great deal with aristocratic families, often used to say that in her bearing and every movement my wife was the greatest aristocrat he had ever seen, and when, in 1906, the workmen made a demonstration demanding free and equal suffrage and secret ballot, my wife walked in their procession.

Charlie was one of eleven children; two were boys, one of them was in business, the elder studied at the University and died young: the girls were very gifted and very independent; two of them are still living and are excellent teachers of music. Each member of the family was of a different faith; each was brought up in religious freedom so that, as he grew up, he could decide about religion for himself. Mr. Garrigue was an agnostic—in those days agnostics were spoken of as atheists—but a man of fine morals, a good husband and father—a real American, bringing up his children to diligence and truthfulness. Charlotte was a Unitarian.

She was beautiful to look at; she had a magnificent intellect, better than mine. It is characteristic of her that she loved mathematics. All through her life her desire was for precise knowledge: but she did not lack feeling on that account. She was deeply religious; death was to her as the passage from one chamber to another, so unshakable was her belief in immortality. In regard to morals she had not a vestige of that moral anarchism which is so widespread in Europe, that is, on the Continent; for that reason, too, she was decided and firm on political and social questions. She was absolutely uncompromising, and utterly truthful: these two qualities had a great influence on my development; through her the best elements of Protestantism became part of my life: that unity of religion and life, practical religion, religion for every day. In those debates we had together in Leipzig, I had got to know her depth: her poets were, like mine, Shakespeare and

121

Goethe, but she saw deeper into them than I did, and could correct Goethe by Shakespeare. We did everything together, we even read Plato together: our whole married life was co-operation. She was very musical: she loved Smetana, and wrote an analysis of his second quartette in my paper *Nase Doba*; she said that that quartette reveals his spiritual unrest. She wrote other studies of his work; perhaps they will be published some day.

I could tell you so much more! Our union was so complete. . . . During the war she fell ill: I had a premonition of it, far away in foreign countries. . . . When I came back to all those celebrations in 1918 I could hardly wait to be beside her.

From American she became Czech, morally and politically. She believed in the genius of our nation, she helped me in my political battles and in all my political activity. I never worked without her co-operation till I was abroad during the war. Even then I knew that I was working in harmony with her. There were many moments when, far away from her, I was acutely aware of our unity of thought. I do not think it was telepathy, but the parallel thinking and feeling of persons who are in complete harmony and who look at the world with the same eyes. She believed that a woman does not live only for her husband, nor a man only for his wife: both must seek the laws of God and fulfil them.

On the Threshold

Yes, my marriage completed my education, my *Lehr-und Wanderjahre*, as I might say, with Goethe. I was twenty-eight. Until 1882 I worked as reader at Vienna University.

I had constant anxiety about making ends meet, and yet bankers came to see me, offering their services for the American millions which I had married. While we were in Klobouky for the holidays a deputation from the whole district came to ask me to have a railway line built from Hustopeč to Klobouky. An ironical situation—but with much humour in it: one citizen of Klobouky came to see us and beat about the bush a long time till at last we extracted from him the admission that he had come to have a look at my wife because, as he said, he had never yet seen—a negress!

The difficulty of making ends meet increased when in my second holidays I fell ill with typhoid fever and returned late to Vienna: but I got lessons, thanks to the help of Mrs. Hartmann, the widow of the revolutionary German writer, Morice Hartmann. Among other things I lectured to a ladies' club at the house of a well-known surgeon, Billroth. My first lectures at the University were on pessimism. During those years as lecturer I felt the spiritual need to deepen my knowledge: I had a wide range, but I needed depth and system. As I have said before, I studied the literature of the leading nations, and attempted a philosophical synthesis both theoretical and practical.

In 1882 the Czech University was founded in Prague, thanks to the active policy of our members of Parliament, and I was appointed to it as Professor of Philology.

As a matter of fact I would rather have had the chair of sociology, but that did not exist in Austria; sociology was recognized at that time as a science in France, England, America, Italy, and elsewhere, but in Germany and Austria learned circles would not even hear of it. In Germany only the philosophy of history was recognized, but its relationship to sociology and history was not clear. Even my thesis on suicide, which had qualified me for a post at the University, belonged, as it were, to no department: one professor of philosophy considered that I should have sent it to the Faculty of Laws, another thought it a socialistic work—it was through the efforts of Brentano and Zimmermann that the University authorities passed it as a qualifying thesis. From the point of view of method, this thesis is the philosophy of history, that is to say, sociology; as far as its subject goes it is an analysis of our great period of transition. Some critics at that time pointed out that I had brought a new subject into the sphere of philosophy, and applauded me for not shirking the burning questions of the day and of life.

That work of mine shows, too, the scientific tendency of my character—synthesis side by side with analysis—yet for all that my opponents in Prague long pronounced me an absolutely analytical, critical, and sceptical spirit. I myself never thought of writing critiques at first: till I left Vienna I wrote none, though newspapers asked for my collaboration. I was preparing my lectures and working out my thoughts very thoroughly: I planned to embody them in a series of theoretical works—but who knows? Nature will not be denied; perhaps I should have turned to practical work even if I had been living abroad. On my arrival in Prague, when I saw the lack of critiques and literature, I devoted myself to detailed critical work in the *Athenaeum*, and published my own newspaper to act as a veritable fireman's douche of ideas. It is possible that I was rather nervy and impatient: I went to Prague really unwillingly, but—*nolentem fata trahunt*. I had allowed matters to develop by themselves, apart from my will. Indeed, I have been drawn into all my battles unwillingly, even when I made mistakes owing to my ignorance of conditions.

In the same way, when I was in politics later on, I had no idea of founding a new political party: it was circumstances which thrust me into public life. Even to-day I appear in public very reluctantly, and only because I must. Of course, once set down before a task I do not shirk it: and what I undertake I carry through to the end.

I am simply giving you bald facts: but my transference to Prague was a fresh crisis for me which I had to live through while still in Vienna. I was afraid of the smallness of Prague; I was an entire stranger to the people and the life of the nation, though I had from time to time come forward as a Czech writer in a modest way. This estrangement from Prague was aggravated to a certain extent by my battle over the manuscripts, and also as a consequence of my political activity. I based nationality and statehood on morality, and for that reason I came in conflict not only with political parties but also with the narrow circle of well-known men who placed so-called nationalism above everything, and regarded it as the motive force of all individual and social life. I see to-day that I was not clear enough even then, and for that reason I made mistakes, not only in practice, but also in theory—but I will talk to you about that another time.

What, is it nearly ten o'clock? I must go and hear the daily report which they make to me. Do you know, from the time I was a blacksmith's apprentice in Čejč I have never stopped working. When I was made President, the German philosopher, Fritz Mauthner, came to visit me: he wanted, he said, to see what a happy man looks like! Happy? Why not? But if I had gone on as a blacksmith at Čejč I might have been just as happy. The great thing is to have a life rich in happenings and inner development—and in that respect I can be satisfied.

Au revoir!

"*Privatdozent*"

Life as a married junior lecturer in Vienna was not easy, but it was worth it! We lived in a room with only a window into a passage, by a curious chance just next door to the house where I had worked as a locksmith's apprentice when I was a boy. We used to cook our breakfast at home; our other meals we got at some cheap little eating house round the corner. Yes, we lived like students and managed all right; but it was difficult when children came.

I was rewriting my thesis on *Suicide*. Before going to America I had presented it as my qualifying thesis for a post at the University, but it had not been found sufficient. I knew that something was lacking, but I had not enough courage yet to say plainly what I meant. Professor Brentano advised me to rewrite it, so I set to work on it again. My wife was very interested in it; it was the first piece of work we did together. And it was this re-written *Suicide* which secured my appointment at the University. It was mainly the philosophy of history, and dealt chiefly with contemporary events. To-day I should formulate it more clearly and fully, but in its essence I should have nothing to alter.

A junior lecturer received no salary, so I earned my living by coaching, and for a short time I had a post as a supplementary professor in a Viennese high school; but I was not a suitable teacher for that type of school. I coached the son of Professor Theodor Gomperz, the philosopher and classical philologist; his son, Harry Gomperz, is now Professor of Philosophy in Vienna. I taught him Latin among other things, coaxing him on by a curious method: I used to give him sentences to translate about something that interested him in his daily life; for instance, if he had figures to add up, he learned them in Latin, and other ways like that. The method worked very well. I gave a lecture on philosophy to a ladies' club at the house of the surgeon Dr. Billroth; there was another club of the same sort at the house of Frau Hartmann, the widow of the German poet from Prague. Altogether my income was small and uncertain, and sometimes I got into difficulties. Oh dear me, yes! The bitterest thing of all was having to borrow money. Once I even borrowed eighty florins from Brentano, which I only repaid him after I got to Prague. Yes, it was very hard to have to borrow; but I thought of my wife whom I could not bear to see in poverty, and that helped me to do it, though I hated it. Once when things were very bad I had a visit from a young Viennese, Herr Oelzelt-Newin, later Lecturer in Philosophy at the University, who wanted to enter the faculty of philosophy, and asked me if I would read philosophy with him, chiefly Kant. He paid me very well. By this time we had two children, Alice and Herbert; I caught typhoid, and my wife got ill too; and then Herr Oelzelt-Newin lent me several thousand florins. Good lord, that seemed a lot of money! I paid him back from Prague.

These difficulties lasted three years, from 1879 till 1882. But after all a man can stand a great deal if he has a taste for work and a sense of duty to his family. This was how I spent my day: in the morning I prepared my lectures and looked up references in the library; twice a week I lectured; in the afternoon I gave private lessons, and in the evenings I rewrote *Suicide* and prepared it for the Press. For social life I had neither time nor inclination.

I knew that there was no chance of my being

appointed professor in Vienna for a long time yet. It was a case of going either to the University of Černovice, or perhaps to Germany. I thought it all out very clearly: if I went to Germany I should become a German writer; I should have to publish German books: but I myself should still remain a Czech, even if only a "lost Czech" like one of our tailors in Berlin or a farmer in Texas. A man remains what he was born. But just about then the Czech University was set up in Prague, and I was invited to go there. So I went.

* * *

Was I glad to go? I was almost sorry. I had certain apprehensions on account of my Czech, and I shrank from the conditions prevailing there in literature and philosophy. I did not know Prague at all; I had only paid a couple of flying visits there. Once when I fetched my pupil Schlesinger from Mariánské Lazně; that evening I looked in at the Arena Theatre where they were playing a stupid farce; after the theatre I went to a café and watched the strange business of prostitution. So my first visit had not made a very good impression on me. The second time I had only spent a night there, on my way back from America to Vienna with my wife. My knowledge of Czech literature was quite unsystematic; at school at Brno there were almost no Czech literary works, and until I came to Vienna I had simply read whatever happened to come my way. I remember in Brno how I used to buy the works of Rubeš, Klicpera, and other elderly gentlemen of that kind, issued in a cheap edition— and compare them to Goethe and Lessing! In Vienna I read Vrchlický and some other poets, but my favourite of them all was Mácha. The academic club held a literary gathering once in a while, but that was not enough. A more stimulating literary influence came from my association with the family of Professor Šembera, especially his daughter Zdenka. The Czechs in Vienna were chiefly work-men, and I had not the time to mix with them systematically. There were a number of Czech officials in the different ministries, but they formed a privileged circle of which as a student I had not the entrée and for which a junior lecturer had no time. I therefore arrived in Prague not knowing a soul, and quite ignorant of Czech life; but I "read myself into" Czech literature and history, and after a while I even managed to penetrate into Czech society. My wife learned Czech, and was convinced that our nation had a mission to fulfil in the world. This was an immense moral support to me, especially as I very soon found myself in opposition to the prevailing opinions around me there.

My wife did not like Vienna. I was accustomed

to the city, for I had lived there twelve years. In the families where I gave lessons I got to know the cultured and liberal Viennese—but I never took root there; I suppose I lacked the real Viennese spirit. Of the cultured people in Vienna, the philosopher Brentano was and remained most akin to me. He was a great man with a mind as keen as a razor. He did not write much, but he had a remarkable influence on his students. I loved his precise, critical faculty, and the way he countered the influence of Herbart, which at that time was practically the official doctrine of aesthetics in Austria; moreover, I had gone through the same conflict with Catholicism as he, on the question of the dogma of infallibility; Brentano did not occupy himself with theology. In his lectures he only propounded arguments in favour of theism. In his work on psychology he promised to give proofs of immortality; but in his lectures, as far as I know, he never touched the subject more closely. I was interested in religion in its whole breadth and scope, and so I travelled quite another road.

But for me, too, the chief event at that time was my loss of faith in the Catholic Church.

In my *Suicide* I have shown how important I consider religion, and especially the loss of faith. I say there that life without faith loses strength

and certainty, and with that I have really said
everything. To-day I could say it better, but in
essence I could not add anything. That is how it
is! I have said already that it was not a masterpiece
—that is not to be expected; I couldn't write it
perfectly even to-day. Yet, do you know, when
that book was published I was denounced as an
atheist. Once while I was studying in Leipzig I
lectured on suicide at the Philosophical Club. Next
day a young men came to me, trembling with
excitement, and told me that for years he had been
possessed by the idea of taking his own life, but
that my lecture had freed him from this *idée fixe*.
In spite of this the clerical and liberal parties
accused me of advocating suicide. I was distressed
at the time that anyone could be so evil-minded.
To-day I am not surprised. The German Catholic
writer, Ratzinger, however, understood at once
that my book was the philosophy of history, and not
an attack on religion. But among the Czechs
Catholicism had not reached this stage of cultural
development, philosophical or theological. In most
cases I had to answer people who did not understand what I was talking about. If people could
understand each other we should have had democracy at one stroke; without mutual understanding,
without tolerance, there is no freedom. Only when
we are completely truthful and open with one

another can we learn to know one another; but without love there is no truth; without truth and love we cannot know our fellows.

Only on this basis can true wedded love be born, clean and strong, the greatest gift in life.

*   *   *

And how, I wonder, can people ask whether woman is man's equal? How should the mother who bore the children not be the equal of the father who begot them? And if a man really loves, how can he love someone beneath him? I see no difference between the intelligence of men and women. When the late Professor Albert wanted to prove to me that women should not study medicine because they have not the muscular or nervous strength to be doctors, I said to him: "Then aren't they too weak to be nurses? A nurse must tend the patient day and night, she must move him and lift him and do everything for him—she needs more strength for that than you surgeons who are operating at most for a couple of hours at a time." And he had nothing to say.

This question of the equality of women is really a problem of the middle classes and intellectuals. In a farmer's or labourer's home the woman must often do the same work as the man, as much work and as heavy work as he. But if the man is sitting in an office it does not occur to him that his wife is having to look after the children, do the marketing, the cooking, cleaning, sewing, and a score of other jobs in the home. I should like to know which of the two does more work! And as for office work, art, science, politics, where women have only just begun to take their place, it is unreasonable and hasty to attempt at this early date to judge whether or no they are fitted for them. And it must be remembered that men have had thousands of years in which to learn these things, and they still do part of their work badly. Besides in the aristocracy they never worried their heads about the equality of women; women became queens and took part in politics as a matter of course.

The underestimation of women is a sign of a polygamous society; and as a matter of fact we are still living in polygamy. Primitive man did not look after his children and treated his wife like a slave or a beast of burden; but he was a warrior, as strong as a wild lion, and he did his part defending the lives of his family with his own life. To-day we are civilized, but, for all that, gross polygamy is maintained. The proof of it lies in the fact of prostitution. And consider how our dual sexual morality works out for men and women, and how it debases marriage. The result, from what I have observed in life and literature, is that in the majority of unsuccessful marriages the fault is the man's. Even where the fault lies with the woman, men are to blame too; for to a large extent they can make whatever they like of their women. I don't mean by that that women are all geniuses and angels; on the whole they are at the same stage of development as men; but they have this merit, that in their life and duties they keep themselves cleaner than men. They don't drink so much or smoke so much, they don't indulge in debauchery—and that is why many a man seeks shelter in marriage.

I see only one way out, and that is education for monogamy. That is a task which has an influence in the field of general culture, to a certain extent an economic and social one, since we cannot combat prostitution without eradicating the degrading poverty which goes with it. If we want morality to increase we must see that folk live beautifully, cleanly, and healthily, that mothers are able to care for their children properly, that folk can earn their living by honest labour. And then there is the drink question, which goes hand in hand with prostitution and poverty in general. I believe that a healthy and intelligent man and woman will not have these complicated modern sex problems. Their relation will be strong, fine, and beautiful. Strong and healthy nature is moral—that is to say, it is never base. That is the hygiene of life, both spiritual and physical. I would not give many moral lectures to young people, but I would say to them: The wellspring of life is only reached by him who in his youth did not lose his feeling for cleanliness. And then—more interest in the children! The majority of fathers these days don't know how to treat their children, and they give very little attention to them. Believe me, the chief lack of our education is a father's influence.

But the greatest argument for monogamy is love. Real love, without limits, the love of one whole being for another, does not pass with age or death. I see it this way: one man, one woman for a whole lifetime; and faithfulness till death. Happy the man or the woman who has been able to live a rigorously monogamous life. Yes, I am for making divorce easier, precisely for this reason: I want marriage to be love, not business or convention, not an unreasonable or thoughtless union. Though of course divorce can be abused like everything else. Love is the great moral strength, the source of all reciprocal sympathy, help, and collaboration; a moral life is an active co-operation in God's order of the world. Love, fellow feeling, united effort; that is the law of life, whether it be for two people, a family, a nation, a State, or a race. I know no other law.

THE MIDDLE YEARS

THE MIDDLE YEARS

Prague

IN the year 1882 I moved to Prague. It happened
in this way. The hypnotist Hansen was giving
demonstrations in Vienna; I went to one of these
and also to visit him. Then some Czech students
asked me if I would lecture to them on the subject
at the Czech students' club. In those days hypnotism
was still looked on as something mysterious and
secret, some kind of "magnetism." I explained
Hansen's experiments psychologically, that is to say
as hypnotism: I lacked the technical knowledge to
explain the hardness of a body under hypnotical
influence. After the lecture Mr. Penížek, who at
that time was one of my students and later became
a journalist, advised me to publish it. He helped
me himself to touch up my rather bad Czech and
sent the manuscript to Prague; it was to have been
published by somebody there, but in the end it
came into the hands of Professors Goll and Hostinský, who were editing a series of lectures in
book form. They published it and drew the attention of Professor Kvíčala to me. Kvíčala was a
member of Parliament, and had taken an influential
part in the founding of the Czech University in

Prague. The outcome of all this was an offer to me to go to Prague as professor-in-extraordinary of philosophy. Kvíčala and the Ministry in Vienna promised me that within three years I should be made professor-in-ordinary, so I went. I found rooms in Karlová Ulice in Smíchov; the windows looked out on to Kinské Gardens. But they got no sun, so I soon moved across the river to Vinohrady Hill above the museum, and a short time after that to Vlček's villa.

A professor-in-extraordinary had a yearly salary of 1,800 florins; I dare say I could have earned something extra by outside employment, but I preferred to be free. We managed to get along somehow; I even had to borrow money sometimes—yes, there were some hard times. After three years I expected to be appointed to the Chair of Philosophy; the proposal for my nomination was already drafted. But I had become entangled, willy nilly, in the manuscript controversy.[1] Some of the professors were against me and for the manuscripts, and so in the ballot on my professorship-in-ordinary there were exactly eleven votes for and eleven against me. The Ministry of Education in Vienna had to decide the question; but with the wisdom of Solomon they left it unsettled; they did not love me either, and they wanted peace in the University.

[1] See note, p. 113.

Would you believe it, somebody in Prague actually lodged a denunciation of me in Vienna, saying that I corrupted youth, that I was a chauvinist, that I repudiated Kant and German philosophy, and I don't know what besides. Archbishop Schönborn and several influential Czechs were against me. Hlávka, the founder of the Czech Academy in Prague, sent to Vienna a copy of my lectures on practical philosophy, in which I had spoken of prostitution and was therefore accused of corrupting youth. Can you imagine a state of things in which it is forbidden to speak to law and philosophy students of such a terrible moral problem as prostitution! Later, when I went to Russia, information was received in Vienna that I was a Russophil and Panslav. That was the kind of thing—well, it no longer makes me angry. It all showed me how lack of freedom can distort people. Of course I was not trusted in Vienna, and that is why I had thirteen years to wait before I was made professor-in-ordinary. By that time Professor Hartl was Minister for Education, and he was so sensible that he did not mind facing jealousy and denunciations.

You see that at first we had plenty of worries. And then, in 1884 or somewhere about then, came the following incident. I had had a pupil in Vienna called Flesch, the son of a well-known Brno manufacturer. He followed me to Prague and continued to attend my lectures. He was a strange, melancholy youth. By and by he went away to Berlin, and there he shot himself. In his will he left me his money. I came to an understanding with his family about it and received a legacy of about sixty thousand florins. That kept me afloat. I was able to pay my debts, help my parents, set up my brother Ludvik in a printing works at Hustopeč, and start the *Athenaeum*—the money didn't last very long! It was said at the time that a suicide had left me his money because I defended the act of suicide.

I have had strange experiences with money. When things were at their worst it has always turned up from somewhere. I have never feared not having enough to eat. I believed that if a man pursued a worthy aim he could not be left without help. As Jesus says: Seek the kingdom of God and everything else shall be added unto you. I am not fond of money; it has never been an end, only a means, whether my object was help for my neighbour or to establish some permanent cultural institution. Perhaps what I like most about my position to-day is that I don't have to carry any money about with me; I have nothing in my pockets but a pencil; I don't even know what Czech money looks like.

* * *

THE MIDDLE YEARS

When I came to Prague I knew no one; I have never had many friends; I don't know how to go half-way to meet people. So I got in touch with the college of professors—Gebauer was the one whom I liked best; he impressed me and I learned method from him. For example, in making notes, he used to jot down each idea on a separate slip of paper, and then file each slip in the drawer where it belonged. He was on the staff of the newspaper *Národní Listy*, and he taught me this about journalism: that it isn't enough to write a thing once in the newspaper; one must repeat it over and over again; a journalist mustn't simply tell himself "So and so has been written and said already," he must say it again in his own words, because readers do not remember what they have read.

I remember how a party of us used to go tramping on Sundays. There was the Sokol Krešl, Professor Kaizl and his uncle, then Professor Heyrovský, the lawyers Marek and Brauner, and perhaps one or two others; we went out together every Sunday on long walks round Prague into the surrounding country; in winter we used to pelt each other with snowballs. All my life I have kept up sports and gymnastics.

One really intimate comrade I had in Prague. That was the painter, Hanuš Schwaiger. He was a good fellow, a tremendously good fellow, with such an inimitable sense of humour which never hurt anyone's feelings and carried him through life and all its hardships without souring him. Sometimes in the evenings I used to go out with him and his friends, the painter Pirner and Professor Klein, the archaeologist from the German University, and drink a glass of beer or wine. And later, when I began to be against alcohol poor old Schwaiger wrote to me—he was very ill by then—saying that I was right, and that he had given up drinking too—because he couldn't manage it any more!

I was in more constant touch with Vojta Náprstek; the link between us was America. I used to go to his reading room "U Halánků," and I lectured there once to a ladies' club on the study of poetry— I developed that lecture later into my little book *On the Study of Poetry*. America was also a link between me and the writer Sládek; he had been in America and I had married an American. I met Julius Zeyer at the "Unionec" or at the house of the Náprsteks; he made a curiously effeminate impression on me. I once met Neruda; he was ill by then and was being taken out for a walk by his servant. He interested me; I had a great regard for him, but I never actually got to know him— perhaps because I had heard that he was on the side of Gregr in the manuscript controversy, but

I don't know if that was true. Sometimes I used to go and watch Bedřich Smetana at the Café Slavia where he was an habitué. Svatopluk Čech I knew a little, and I wrote an article for his magazine *Blossoms*. He was a shy, timid creature; even in his poetry I could feel his inability to face facts; even in *The Songs of a Slave* his satire is quite impersonal, general, vague.

And at the University? Well, at first of course the most important person was Kvíčala, and then Tomek; I had more to do with the younger ones, Gebauer, Goll, and Hostinský. The full number of professorial chairs was not yet complete. A kind of social aristocracy was formed by the sons of the great nationalists of the previous generation. Čelakovský's son, a botanist, Frič, Palacký's son, a geographer, who used to be called "the runaway encyclopaedic dictionary." The students were brought up in the liberalism of those days; my inaugural lecture was on "Hume and Scepticism"— it created quite a sensation that I chose a subject from English philosophy, even translating passages to my students and criticizing the problem of scepticism. University circles were not pleased by my criticism of Kant and German pro-Kantian philosophy—another unhappy instance of ex- aggerated anti-German patriotism linked with actual dependence on Germany. When one of the students' clubs asked me to lecture I spoke on Blaise Pascal, and showed them, from him, that religion is not dead, as German liberalism would have it, but that it is a necessity of the human heart. I fought against all that liberalist indifference. To the cultivated men of those days religion was an exploded fallacy, and they could hardly understand how a man could seriously give his attention to it.

I did not care much for teaching: I almost disliked lecturing. I am not fond of speaking in public, and have even to force myself to write. I was not interested in explaining to my students what other people had already written and taught; I said to them, "There are such and such books on these subjects; you had better read them." I preferred to discuss concrete and present-day problems with them; and I liked it best of all when they asked me questions or argued with each other in my presence. At least that showed me that they were thinking, and what they were thinking, and it made all sorts of things clearer to me as well. When it couldn't be done in the lecture room I took them home with me. But I found the teaching itself very hard sometimes. Think what a responsibility it is to instruct young people in moral questions. Yes, to teach a boy to read and write, hand out general knowledge to him, and explain what has already been discovered and written is a very different matter from assuming responsibility for the actions of those who listen to you, taking you as their example, and acting in accordance with your words. Then you are responsible for their lives, whether you are teacher or writer. Sometimes when I was going to lecture and had actually got as far as the University buildings I would be overcome with such a feeling of moral depression that I couldn't go on—I simply couldn't. I would turn back home and send a message to my students by the porter that I was unable to lecture that day.

Perhaps the real reason why I have never been a good pedagogue is that all my life I have only been educating myself. I am an individualist and a democrat, both in life and in metaphysics. I believe that all souls are equal; each soul belongs to itself, is independent and a law unto itself. Folk develop side by side, each for himself; they cannot really influence one another except as friends who understand each other. The main thing is to look after oneself, to control and perfect oneself, and leave others to do the same. That is not egoism; on the contrary. To be independent, self-reliant, and self-sufficing really means that one does not demand of other people things that one can and should do for oneself. For there is moral beggary as well as material. I have always wanted each one of us to be his own master. This applies to politics, social life, and morals. To be one's own master; that includes both liberty and discipline.

*   *   *

There are not many of us left who can clearly remember the 'eighties in Prague. You think to-day that those were great days, because you measure them by the great names of those days, Rieger, Neruda, Vrchlický; but at the time we were often hampered by petty customs, petty means, and petty people. . . . As I always say, when I am worried by the limitations of to-day, perhaps in fifty years our times will appear to the people living then in such a blaze of splendour that they will almost envy us.

I am not an admirer of "the good old days." Sometimes when I think that we ought to return to the ideals of our fathers I remind myself of what those times were like, and tell myself that we are nearer to their ideals to-day. The world is better than it was then; in particular our Czech world has gained tremendously. I would punish everyone who complains of the present day by transporting him back into the 'eighties. I have lived long enough to say that I believe in the future, in evolution and progress. I should like to see how life will be a hundred years hence.

Since the war I have slept badly, and I don't

care always to read half the night; it's bad for the eyes. So I paint Utopias of the world as it will be in twenty or a hundred years. They are practical Utopias; I look for the best that there is to-day, and embroider it a little. The future is with us now; if we choose the best things in our life to-day we should be on the right road—we should have amplified our life with a bit of the future.

Many Conflicts

On my appointment to Prague I had only a professorial career in mind; I was afraid that conflicts might arise, but I would much rather have avoided them. It is not true that I am a fighter by nature. I never wanted to be in the forefront of all sorts of political affairs and polemics; usually it was other people who dragged me into them.

I found a rather poor standard at the new Czech University, no exercise of criticism, no exchange of opinions. Once Professor Durdík gave a lecture to the philosophical society, in which he told his listeners to name those whom they considered the five greatest philosophers. He asked for discussion, but no one stood up to speak. So I said that he must not omit Comte. At that there was consternation at the spectacle of a professor-in-extraordinary opposing a professor-in-ordinary. The students had a lot of fun out of it, and shortly afterwards Durdík answered me sarcastically in the Press, saying that an American like myself would probably declare Barnum to be the greatest philosopher.

Because I saw that we needed an organ of expert criticism I founded the monthly *Athenaeum*; it contained reviews of our own and foreign scientific works, and also literary criticism—for me literature has always been as important a source of knowledge as science. Professor Pacl of the technical college published a book on architecture; one of his colleagues wrote a most crushing review of it in the *Athenaeum*; and I, as editor, had a disagreeable time over it. The author, Jerábek, who wrote the play *The Servant of His Master*, presented a thesis on romantic poetry as candidate for the Chair of Literature; again in a joint work of some of his colleagues in the *Athenaeum* it was maintained that his book was scientifically weak. I had no idea that Jeřábek was a protégé of Rieger; but Rieger saw in the criticism an insult to himself, and was offended with me about it. One more illustration of how things were then: a certain University professor found fault with the *Athenaeum* for reviewing new and foreign books; it didn't do, it appeared, for the students to read of material on their subject before the professor had quoted it in his lectures, that undermined the lecturers' authority of the professor. The *Athenaeum* continued to appear for about ten years; it was far from being a really good review, but it was at least something.

And I noticed that our new University needed to take more trouble about popular culture; so I proposed that it should arrange an extension course for the widest circles; and I myself delivered such a series of lectures. I wrote that we must have a second Czech University. I saw, too, that we needed an encyclopaedic dictionary. Rieger's dictionary had been good in its day, but had got out of date. I wanted a scientific encyclopaedia, something like the *Encyclopaedia Britannica*, so I found collaborators and a publisher. But the controversy over the manuscripts upset my work; and besides I had ideas which the others found it difficult to accept. For example, I proposed that my colleagues on the dictionary should work as hard as they could for a whole year, and then burn all they had written —I considered that we needed practice and experience. Well, the practical result of my plans has at least been Otto's *Encyclopaedic Dictionary*, and while preparing it I met at the Ottos' house Mr. Laichter, who later published the *Selected Didactic Essays* and the magazine *Our Era*. I also wanted to publish our old religious memorials, the writings of Huss, Stítny, Chelčický, and others; it seemed to me not enough to boast about our Hussite past; we needed to know it. A club was even founded for this purpose, but it did not get as far as publishing the things . . . I think because of the manuscript business.

It would never have occurred to me to take part in the controversy if Gebauer, with whom I had had very little to do at that time, had not come to me and asked me to print in the *Athenaeum* an article in which he proved that the so-called Dvora Králova and Hora Zelená manuscripts were fabrications of our own century. I think it happened in this way: Gebauer had explained his objections to the manuscripts in some literary review or other, and Martin Hattala attacked him for it in the Press; so now Gebauer wanted to defend himself. It is true that Kvíčala and Gebauer had a *Philological Review* of their own, but Kvíčala would not publish it there, for fear of offending his collaborators. Of course I accepted the article, partly because I knew what a scholar Gebauer was, and partly because I did not myself believe in the authenticity of the manuscripts. I had already been influenced to a certain extent in the matter by Šembera in Vienna, and still more by the criticisms of Vašek. To me the question of the manuscripts was first and foremost a moral question: if they were forgeries we must confess it before the whole world. Our pride, our culture, must not be based on a lie. Besides, we could not truly get to know our own real history while we were obsessed by a fancied past. The case seemed perfectly obvious to me.

The result of this was a controversy which lasted for years. Philologists, historians, paleographers, chemists, declared that the manuscripts were false; I tried to prove ethnically and sociologically that they could not come from the Middle Ages. Hattala opposed us; Kvíčala, who had told Gebauer in confidence that he didn't believe in the authenticity of the manuscripts, turned against us too; then the newspapers attacked us, decrying us as unpatriotic and traitors to our nation. It was all very silly. The clubs began to take up the question, and even the man in the street. One day I was in a beer house waiting for Schwaiger; at the next table was Vojta Naperstek's brother, the proprietor. He didn't know who I was, and began talking about me, saying that I was paid by the Germans to belittle the past of the Czechs, etc. I let him go ahead and even led him on; it was only after I had left the place that the others told him he had been talking about me to myself. Another time I joined with some folk in a tram in cursing that traitor Masaryk. I found it very amusing; what made me angry was to see that some of them were not honest in defending the manuscripts; they did not believe in them, but were afraid to confess it.

The whole affair had one excellent result for me: I had to read the whole literature of the period which really gave rise to the manuscripts. I read the whole of the literature of the nationalist revival through and through, from Dobrovský onwards— a great fellow, Dobrovský,[1] the first cultivated Czech of that new era with a world-wide outlook. I read Jungmann, Linda, and Šafařík. And by the way, the defenders of the manuscripts extolled the old pagan era, unspoiled by German influence, yet they joined with us in honouring Saint Wenceslas![2] We have our mouths full of tradition, but as for recognizing it—no. I went all through the literature of the eighteenth and nineteenth centuries carefully,

[1] Dobrovský (1753–1829) was the most important personality in the early Czech patriotic revival.

[2] Saint Wenceslas was Duke of Bohemia for nine troubled years (920–929) when the country was rent by quarrels between Christians and pagans. Catholicism at that date meant accepting the influence and domination of the Holy Roman Empire, to which the Pagan Party in Bohemia, led by Wenceslas' brother and brother's wife, fiercely objected. Wenceslas had been educated as a Christian and it is possible that he also saw that more was to be gained by friendliness with his powerful German neighbours than by continual wars with them. He finally averted a war with Henry the Fowler, Duke of Saxony, by consenting to pay him annual tribute, and this so incensed the Pagan Party in his country that they had him murdered on September 28, 929. He was canonized. September 28th is still celebrated as a great festival at which Czechs honour him as a Czech saint and Germans as a friend of Germany.

to get a good idea of the period surrounding the origin of the manuscripts, and the mood out of which they sprang; and I found romanticism, historicism, the yearning to compete with other nations, especially with Germany. Through the manuscript controversy I got to know our movement for national revival; I was led far into the past, right back into our history, to the Reformation and counter-Reformation; and forward again to the leaders of the national awakening, Palacký, Kollár, Smetana, Havlíček. So that even for me the controversy was a political event; it introduced me to our political problems.

*   *   *

Soon after that there was another rumpus. I had invited a young man to come to Prague, Hubert Gordon Schauer, the son of a mixed Czech-German marriage; he was a young Hegelian, and had got into trouble in Vienna. Dr. Zaba, the Professor of Philosophy, recommended him to me, saying that it was a pity that he should be involved in such difficulties, and that I ought to protect him for the sake of the Czech nation. Well, that was all right. I persuaded him to come to Prague and I put him up at our house; I was living then at Vaclav Vlček's villa on Vinohrady. Schauer turned out to be a gifted youngster, but unbalanced; he indulged in late nights and every kind of spree; and then one night he got in by climbing over the fence, trampled Vlček's flower beds, and made an awful mess; so I had to turn him out. Just about then the group of young students round us younger professors wanted to have a newspaper of their own, and founded the fortnightly magazine *Time*. I knew nothing about it till I saw the first number, and in it I found an article by Schauer, "Our Two Problems." I think they must have put it in because they hadn't enough contributions to fill the paper. It was an impossible thing: the author demanded anonymously whether it would not be better for us Czechs to throw in our lot with the Germans and join in the life of a great cultured nation. I thought matters over, and then early next morning I went to have it out with Herben, who edited the paper. To this day I remember how I found him in bed under one of those enormously thick down quilts that you see in the country. And I told him what I thought of him. But that didn't prevent my being blamed for the article. One writer hurled a national curse at me in *Narodní Listy* as the philosopher of suicide, and the kindly poetess Krasnohorská, who was nothing if not thorough, even cursed my mother. Later Schauer freely admitted his authorship of the article, and was even taken on to the staff of the very newspaper that had been abusing me; but the fury roused against me took a long time to die down.

*   *   *

It seemed to be by chance that I was hurled into these conflicts, but I now see that my surroundings were always drawing me into public affairs, and that even in my lectures I sought to influence them. For instance, in lecturing on Hume, Pascal, and Comte I was trying deliberately to turn people's attention to English and French philosophy and win them from their one-sided intellectual subservience to Germany. That was why I had a shortened version translated and published of Comte's *Sociologie* and Sully's *Psychology*. My own *Concrete Logic*, hurriedly written during holidays at Hustopeč, was an attempt to bring order and method into the sciences; even in science each specialist goes hurrying along in his own groove, having nothing in common with his neighbours, and just as strangers pass in the street; and all organization, all overcoming of anarchy is by nature political.

*   *   *

My greatest interest at this time was the Slavic question. I had thought about it, rather vaguely perhaps, while I was still a child. As a boy I had cudgelled my brains to find out how it was that I could understand what the Polish lancers said (they had a camp for a time at Čejkovice) though they belonged to another nation. While I was still at school I learnt Polish out of romantic sympathy with the Polish rebellion; and in Vienna I studied Russian.

Once as a boy I spent my holidays in Hungary, staying on a farm near a castle, not far from Lake Balaton. I was fascinated by the study of some historical atlases, trying to work out how far north-east the Roman Empire had extended, how deep the empire of Svatopluk had penetrated into Pannonia and wherever Slavs had settled. By guesses and calculations I worked out that Székesfehérvár[1] was the ancient Velehrad of Svatopluk, and made other amusing conjectures. One morning I was sitting before the castle absorbed in one of my atlases when a gentleman came up and began to talk to me. The longer he talked the more technical he became, and in the end he tore my Slav fantasies all to pieces. He was the famous paleographer and historian from Vienna University, Professor Sickel, and had come on a visit to the owner of the castle.

I had "read myself into" Russian literature while I was still in Vienna; later, in Prague, it absorbed me altogether. I may tell you that hardly anyone

[1] A town about mid-way between Budapest and Lake Balaton.

at that time had such a good knowledge of Russian literature as I. In the writings of Kollár I came upon Slavophilism, and there were Slavophiles still in our political life; but I saw that they only paid lip service to their creed of Slavism without really understanding it. So I studied the Russian Slavophiles: Kiryeyevsky, the disciple of Schelling, and especially Dostoyevski. I learnt from them how Russian Slavophilism is linked with Orthodoxy. Dostoyevski was an atheist; he himself said once to the Russian nihilists: "You will tell *me*, what is atheism?" But he *wanted* to be orthdox; he wanted to "give the lie to truth." Vain hope. No man can return to his lost faith; he can accept a new one, but the one that he has lost he never finds again. For this reason I felt something akin to Jesuitism in this longed-for orthodoxy of Dostoyevsky. I was not satisfied with it; I wanted to see Russia and the Orthodox faith at close quarters.

I went to Russia for the first time in 1887, and again a year later. I stayed in Warsaw to get to know the Poles; I visited Petersburg, Moscow, Kiev, and Odessa: it fascinated me to see so many streets and places which I knew so well from Dostoyevski, Tolstoi, and other Russian writers. I went third class on the train and between decks on the Black Sea, partly because I wanted to get to know the people and partly because I had not much money. I got in touch with some Slav philologists; one of them, Lamanskiy, told me straight out that the Russians are only interested in the orthodox Slavs and most of all in the Slovaks, because they are just as simple as the religious folk in Russia; the liberal and western Czechs they would send to the devil. I went into the Russian churches and visited shrines and hermitages. At the Sergyeyev Monastery I was the guest of the Father Igumen; I noticed the lack of culture and the superstition of Orthodox Russians, and remembered with surprise that it was to them that the Slavophiles looked to protect Slavism. On the whole I left the country with the same feelings as Havlíček before me: love for the Russian people and dislike of the official policy and the ruling intelligentsia.

I called on Tolstoi. I had not had the opportunity to read him as thoroughly as I had Dostoyevski, so I wanted to know him personally. I visited him first in Moscow in his palace. I remember as if it were to-day how he showed me his workshop with an air almost of pride; it had a wooden ceiling like a farm kitchen, and so low that I could touch it with my hand; but the ceiling had been artificially added to one of the high palace rooms. In this room there was a writing desk, a comfortable leather arm-chair, and a divan—in their rustic setting they looked decidedly unsuitable. He had a wooden clock from the Black Forest which he calculated only cost thirty-five kopecks. He wore a belted shirt like a *mujik*, and boots which he had sewn himself—it goes without saying that they were badly sewn. He took me to drink tea in the reception rooms, all upholstered in red velvet as was the custom in the houses of the nobles. The Countess passed him the usual jam, but as if he had not noticed it he sipped his tea through a piece of sugar like the *mujiks*. After tea we went into the park; we talked of Schopenhauer, whom Leo Nikolaievitch did not understand very well; in the middle of our conversation he stopped like a *mujik* at the boundary of his field and invited me to come and see him again—it all seemed to me affected, artificially primitive, unnatural.

Later on Leo Nikolaievitch invited me to Yasnaya Polyana. I went from the town of Tula by the *Kibitka*. In front of the village was a little bridge so broken that the horses would have shaken it to bits with their hoofs; we had to make a detour. Some time before noon I arrived at Tolstoï's house; I was told that Leo Nikolaievitch was still asleep because he had been debating all the night with Tchernov and some guests. So I went for a turn through the village, which was dirty and poverty-stricken. A young *mujik* was working in front of a cottage; I began to talk to him, and I saw that under his ragged shirt he had some sores—venereal disease. In another hut I found an old woman baking in the dirt and without help, working on till she died. I went back to Tolstoi's house. That day his young disciple, Gay, the son of the painter, arrived to see him; this young man had emancipated himself to such an extent that he came on foot from far away to see Tolstoi, because he said the railway was not peasant-like; he arrived in such a lousy condition that he had to go at once and have a good bath and scrub. Tolstoi told me himself that he would drink from the same glass as a syphilitic so as not to show his disgust and not to humiliate him; he thought of that but he did not think of ridding his peasants of the infection. And when he began explaining to me that we ought to live the simple life, the life of a peasant, I said to him: "What about your house, with its reception room, and its arm-chairs and divans? And what about the wretched, poverty-stricken life of your peasants? Is that the simple life? It's true you don't drink, but you smoke cigarette after cigarette. If we are to have asceticism, then let it be thorough. The peasant lives wretchedly because he is poor, but not for the sake of asceticism," And I told him what I had seen in his village, the disorder, disease, and dirt. "How in God's name can you fail to see it?" I asked him. "You are a great artist; don't you

164

know how to observe? To sew one's own boots, to go on foot instead of travelling by train, all that is only time thrown away; think of all the useful things you could have been doing in it!" I quoted him the English proverb "Cleanliness comes next to godliness" and our Czech proverb "Cleanliness is the half of health." But the long and the short of it was that we couldn't understand each other. The Countess was a sensible woman and hated to see the unreasonable way in which Tolstoi gave away everything he had; she thought of her children. In her quarrel with Leo Nikolaievitch later I could not help feeling her in the right.

The third time I visited Tolstoi was shortly before his death in 1910; by that time he was inwardly completely separated from his wife. He was very nervous and uncontrolled. The village doctor, who attended him, was a Czech called Makovický. He was unreasoningly devoted to Tolstoi and his teaching; he carried a piece of pencil-lead stuck in his finger-nail with which he wrote down in a note-book in his hip-pocket all that Leo Nikolaievitch said without his seeing. Simplicity! The simple life! My God! The problem of town and country cannot be solved by a sentimental morality and a declaration that the farmer and rural life are the pattern for all. Agriculture to-day is becoming industrialized; it cannot be

165

left without machinery, and the farmer needs more education than his grandfather did. There are still many false ideas and inherited prejudices on this subject in our country too.

Most of all we disagreed about non-resistance to evil. He did not understand that the question is not merely to oppose evil by force, but to wage war against it all along the line; he did not see the difference between defensive and offensive; he thought, for example, that if the Russians had not resisted their Tartar invaders they would, after a short period of slaughter, have desisted from violence. My theory was this: If a man attacks me and tries to kill me I shall defend myself, and unless someone comes to the help of the bully, I shall kill him; if one of us has got to be killed, let it be the one who originated the evil thought.

* * *

I have no more use for empty talk about Slavism than I have for flag-wagging patriots. I wonder how many of our Slavophiles can even read Russian, Polish, and Serb? They are just like the folk who are always proclaiming that we are the nation of Huss. How many of them have read even a page of Huss, or even one book on the Hussite Reformation? And in any case, what's the use of talking? A normal individual does not go about trumpeting

166

abroad the fact that he loves his parents, his wife, his children; that is taken for granted. If you love your country don't talk about it, but do something worth while; that is all that matters. I know well enough what a great but at the same time difficult programme is presented by Slavism. I have studied in Poland, I have studied in Russia, I have been active in politics among the Croats and Serbs; I am more than half Slovak, and fifty years ago I had a Slovak programme. Of course I didn't do all that without loving my country; man is so made that he is glad to follow his heart; that is why he does not speak of love but looks for help to his reason. I was always held back by a kind of shame from saying the words "my country," "my nation." . . . I don't cry aloud that I am a patriot, and I don't cry out against another for being a traitor to his country; I must patiently prove that his way is wrong for such and such reasons. These mighty slogans can make folk drunk but they cannot teach them to work. We have freed ourselves from our despotic masters, but we still have to free ourselves from the despotism of words. Folk cling to words not only in politics but in all subjects, religion, science, philosophy. That is why I have always laid emphasis on things, on observing and recognizing facts; but to observe and recognize really well —that needs love.

Politics

Politics have always interested me. Even the village feuds between Slovaks and Hanaks and later between the Czech and German boys at Brno, were politics in miniature; I had to become aware of the terms between Czechs and Germans. Even my desire to go to the Consular Academy was only half romantic; it was half a cloudy interest in politics. My relation to them was first only theoretical; Plato had fascinated me by his political philosophy, and as soon as I took up sociology I was inevitably plunged into political problems. Economics fascinated me too; I attended lectures by famous economists in Vienna and Leipzig, and as a student I dipped into the second edition of Marx's *Capital*.

Of course I always reacted to political events. While I was still a student I wrote my first article for the *Moravian Eagle*, condemning the policy of passivity. In Vienna I went to the railway station to watch the arrival of the Czech members of Parliament. I was continually studying the conflict between Czechs and Germans; but I understood that it was really a struggle against Austria, and my attitude to Austria was rather negative.

When I first came to Prague I was full of cultural and scientific interests; the *Athenaeum*, the University, the encyclopaedia, the manuscript controversy, and rising out of that, journalistic and political activity. My study of the fictitious ancient Slav culture became a study of the whole cultural life of my own time. Then the magazine *Time* was founded without any activity on my part, and there was the fuss about Schauer. These conflicts and polemics really drew me into active politics. I recognized our mistakes, the low standard of our journalism and public opinion, but I found decent and fine people as well. It was even good for me that, often against my will and sometimes from sheer stupidity, I roused such fury and hostility. At the time I said to myself: "You deserve it all for getting yourself mixed up in such things!" But to-day I see that even by arousing such hatred one becomes famous and respected. The hatred passes, but one's name remains in people's heads. Even to-day I still say this to those who have to defend themselves on all sides.

We formed a little group of professors: Kaizl, Kramař, to a certain extent Heyrovský and Rezek, and they even said Goll was one of us. But that was not true. We had nothing that you could call a political programme; it was more that we held together as a generation. We wanted to improve the state of things, to reform the Press and the University; we were for a positive and active policy, a general direction rather than a clear-cut programme, a line of critical and scientific thought. Kaizl was an economist and Kramař was writing an excellent book on the activities of the Czech Court Office in Vienna, abolished under Maria Theresa. Pazdírek wrote about our group in his *Slawische Warte*, and gave me the article to read in manuscript; I saw that he called us "positivists," and that reminded me too much of Comte and French positivism, so I told Pazdírek that he had better say "realists." That is how we came by the name.

Pazdírek wanted to get us into the Old Czech Party, and negotiated about it with Rieger; he promised him more from us than we could perform, he was such a naïve, good-natured fellow. Now I was friends with Bráf, who knew Rieger's family, so he introduced me to Rieger and Mattuš and they began to negotiate with us about joining the Old Czechs. Rieger was very nice to me in spite of our former differences, and we got on well together. We had ready a statement of the conditions on which we would join the Party: we demanded that we should exercise the main influence on the Party Press; but this was not to the liking of the Old Czech journalists, and they began to get their knives into us, in particular the staff of *Voice of the Nation*. So the attempt came to nothing.

Then in about 1889 the Young Czechs had their

victory at the polls. In reality there was not such a great difference between them and the Old Czechs as one might have thought from their skirmishes in the Press. Even in our little group of realists there were some who thought along Old Czech lines. I used to say that Kaizl was an Old Czech Realist, Kramař was a Young Czech Realist, and I was a realistic Realist. The Young Czechs were gaining votes, so they needed new people to enter Parliament. They negotiated with us about entering their Party, and we debated whether it was our duty to put ourselves at their disposal. The Old Czechs had on the whole better people, and were more cultivated, but politically they were unprogressive. Dr. Jan Kučera, the lawyer, was active in furthering our adherence to the Young Czechs, so was Škarda, a member of the Diet with whom I was on friendly terms. So we joined that Party. A fair-minded statement in *National News* and *Time* wiped out our former enmity; and at the next elections to Parliament—that was in 1891—I was elected as member of the Young Czech Party for the district of Domažlice.

The spiritual leader of the Young Czech Party was Dr. Engel, a physician; he drew up every agenda, and was a very excellent and sensible man, but he kept too much in the background, and appeared little in public. Then there were the two

Grégrs. Dr. Julius Grégr lived in Prague, and was director of *National News*; Dr. Edward Grégr was a member of Parliament and an orator, an excellent fellow, but sometimes his temperament led him away into flights of exaggerated radicalism till the welkin rang; he himself had to laugh about it afterwards. There was the patriarch Trojan, a former Old Czech, a simple and dignified man; there was Dr. Herold, who certainly deserved his name; he was a magnificent orator, the herald and standard-bearer of the Party; and Ervin Špindler, a newspaper man with a heart of gold and an apostolic beard—I used to have debates with him on liberalism and atheism; he could not understand how an educated man could be religious. Among the radicals was Vašatý, the brother of my former teacher at the school at Hustopeč. This Vašatý led the Slav policy, though he had not much knowledge of Slavism. He had no confidence in us, and when I had a conflict with the Party he sided against me. On the whole we realists were well received by them all; only the Vienna correspondent of *National News*, Eim, was annoyed every time I had any success in Parliament. He began by being strongly in favour of me but soon began to behave rather unpleasantly.

What interested me most of all in the Vienna Parliament was the Parliament itself. I had read the Constitution and Rules of Procedure through carefully again and again, but between the constitutional form and the parliamentary practice there is as great a difference as between the Gospels and the Church. I kept my eyes open and my thoughts to myself. The Government tribune looked to me like an altar; we down below were supposed to be the believers. I soon discovered that there was a fine library in the Parliament; I did not neglect it among the quantities of meetings, and there I read political literature. I was still immature and inexperienced in politics; as an orator I had some success; I spoke on education, in the Delegations, the joint committee of the Austrian and Hungarian Parliaments which dealt with Foreign Affairs, I led an attack against the Minister Kállay on the Bosnia Herzegovina question; that had the advantage of winning me the friendship of the Croat and Serb members of Parliament. I travelled through Bosnia Herzegovina, watched by Kállay's spies. Once I annoyed the German member, Menger, so much that he called me a traitor; there was a great fuss about that; Menger was reprimanded and had to apologize to me before the whole House.

After a number of differences I came into conflict with the Party. It happened like this. The first time that I spoke to Lieutenant Thun in Parliament at Prague he expressed himself very insultingly about the Czechs, and said that a Czech is either a lout or a toady. Naturally I mentioned this remark of his to various people, and it got into the Press, and there was a dreadful row about it; I was reproached by the people in the Party with not having told them what had happened—as a matter of fact I had spoken about it to Dr. Tilscher, but he had obviously forgotten. In connection with this affair an anonymous and very bitter article attacking Julius Grégr appeared in *Time*. Grégr thought that it was written by me so he went for me. I told no one the real author's name, and preserved editorial secrecy. Not even Dr. Kramař knew. It was only lately, after all these years, that it became known that the article was by Kaizl. In the Party, of course, it was nasty; they settled the matter with an unsalted and unbuttered declaration which could only point to me, though it did not mention me directly. I went to my electors, got a vote of confidence from them, and with that satisfaction in my pocket wrote to our representative in Vienna laying down my mandate. Perhaps I should have consulted my colleagues in our group beforehand, but I often made up my mind on the spur of the moment. Kaizl and Kramař remained in the Party. I disliked the policy of the Young Czech Party because of its ambiguity: it was one thing in Prague and another in Vienna; at home the members of Parliament

protested thunderously, while in Vienna the
Government bound them by small concessions. My
attitude to the Germans differed from the Party's
as well. But the chief thing I had learnt was that I
was still weak in politics.

My resignation did not mean that I renounced
politics; on the contrary. I wanted to begin from
the foundations; I wanted to make a new policy, a
policy of the future, and to impress myself on the
thought of our people. I devoured the whole of
political literature from the eighteenth century onwards. The personality I liked most was Dobrovský,
with his keen intellect and world outlook; my
political teacher was Palacký; my humanitarian
programme was based on his teaching. I admired
Havlíček for his sincerity and openness; he was my
model in journalism. The fruit of these studies of
mine was my book *The Czech Question*, a hurried
piece of work, really only a collection of material; I
also got the idea for my books on *Havlíček* and *Our
Present-Day Crisis*.

It was always like that with me; I should so
much have liked not to have to publish books; I
never polished and perfected them enough. When
I published them it was only because I felt that
they had a topical importance. If folk had left me
alone—and I them—I daresay I should never have
published a single volume. When I had joined the

fray I laid about me, but I never struck an unnecessary blow. I hurt people, it is true, but I got more than I gave. I often overlooked people; and I used to be vain. But my chief fault was impatience. I felt that people should accept truth at once and act on it. I have had fights all my life, but I don't believe that I'm pugnacious by nature. I never fought for the sake of fighting; it was rather that I was attacked and defended myself. A literary battle is quite useful for some things; it may make one blind but it causes one to think and one's adversary too. I believe that all these conflicts really contributed to the national consciousness and to intensification of our spiritual life.

*   *   *

It is strange, considering what quantities of books and pamphlets I published, that I published them all unwillingly. And as I told you a little while ago, I had no inclination for teaching either. And believe me, I dislike appearing in public. If I could have followed my own inclinations in my life, I would have been satisfied to read, study, and perhaps write for my own information; in short, *to learn*. There is nothing that does not interest me: all sciences, all problems and tasks of our day. I am happy if I can read in quiet, and I am a voracious reader to this day. I don't like meeting new

176

people; I am shy of them; each acquaintance, even a formal one, is a piece of work for me. All this has made politics and public activity harder for me than for many others. Why did I do it then? Because I had to; of course that is easily said, but if I say it it is not an excuse or an apology. You see from all my books, pamphlets, and articles, from all my work, that I have never interfered in matters which were not important and topical and which were not part of the problem of my own life. Since I came to Prague in 1882 I have been collecting more and still more experience. I am grateful to Fate for the fullness of my life.

The 'Nineties

When I look back on the 'nineties now I see what a time of ferment it was. And of course I do not reckon the period 1890–1900 to the minute. Just consider the disintegration in the political parties. Up to that time we had really only had two parties, the Old Czechs and the Young Czechs. Then the Old Czech Party degenerated; it was the decline of the old bourgeois patricians; the Young Czechs were rather the Party of the new, rising class, more rural and radical. Between 1889 and 1891 the Young Czechs had a majority over the Old Czechs in the Diet and in Parliament. Till then our whole policy had been what I should call bourgeois to-day, but in the 'nineties it began to split up and differentiate itself socially. The philosopher Alfons Štastný organized agrarianism within the ranks of the Young Czechs; he was one of your popular sophists, an atheist, and a disciple of German materialism as expounded by Vogt, Moleschott, and Büchner; I laughed at his ideas, and I suppose that is why he was so angry with me. Then there was Socialism. In actual fact we had it earlier; one can trace its tentative beginnings as far back as 1848; we had had some Christian Socialism, but gradually, as industry developed, there came the rise of the working class; it was in the 'nineties that under the influence of the Viennese Socialists a strong Social Democratic Party began to grow up on the basis of Marxism. Klofáč organized the Nationalist Workers to oppose them in the Young Czech Party; but they soon split off from the Party and began to act for themselves. I came into active conflict with some of them.

Socialism has interested me all my life. While I was in Brno I observed Christian Socialism, and in Vienna I read Marx and the writings of the Catholic Socialists. Later in Vienna Vogelsang was the prominent Christian Socialist. When my friend Hanuš Schwaiger painted St. George at the

178

castle at Pruhonice I visited him there and met
Count Sylva Taroucca, whom I had known in
Parliament; and at his house I met the German
Christian Socialist, Dr. Mayer.

During the 'nineties I began to come into practical contact with Socialism; I went about among
the labourers and lectured to them. When there
were strikes in Prague and in Kladno I arranged
courses of lectures, and lectured myself to the
strikers. I wanted to divert their thoughts so that
they would not have only hunger and poverty in
their heads. I suggested the foundations of a
"Workers' Academy" where the workmen and
those who wrote in their newspapers could get some
education in politics. During the campaign for
universal suffrage in 1905 I addressed a public
meeting at Senovážné Náměstí,[1] and when they
made their demonstration I walked with my wife
in their procession. Even before then I had been
accused of Socialism in speeches and articles, and
I was always caricatured wearing the Socialist
slouch hat. In those days the word "Socialist" was
like a red rag to a bull to the middle classes and
intellectuals. I accepted Socialism as far as it coin-
cided with my humanitarian programme; Marxism
I did not accept. My book *The Social Question* was

[1] The old hay market in Prague, one of the largest squares, now
called Havlíčkovo Náměstí.

179

based on my criticism of Marx. When the Czech Socialists entered the Vienna Parliament they refused to join in the declaration of constitutional rights made by the other Czech parties. There was a great outcry against them because of that, and they were accused of betraying their country; I stood up for them, and of course I got attacked as well, although the founders of the Young Czech Party had invoked not only historical but national rights just as I was doing then.

* * *

My Socialism is simply love of one's neighbour, of humanity. I want to abolish poverty, and enable everyone to be able to live by his work and in his work; give everyone enough elbow-room, as the Americans say. Humanitarianism is not the old style philanthropy; philanthropy only helps here and there, but real love of humanity seeks to amend the state of things by process of law. If that is Socialism, so much the better.

In equality—absolute equality—I do not believe. Neither in stars nor in men is there equality. There always have been and always will be individuals who by their own gifts and a combination of extraneous circumstances beyond their control, can and do achieve more than others; there will always be a hierarchy among men. But hierarchy means order,

180

organization, discipline, knowledge, and obedience, not the exploitation of man by man. That is why I do not accept Communism. Lenin, as soon as he was in power, began to summon leading personalities. The longer I live the more I realize the true rôle of the individual in the evolution of humanity. But I repeat, higher gifts and so-called good fortune are no justification for the exploitation of the less gifted and fortunate. I do not believe that one can do away with all private ownership. The personal relation, that real "price of affection," which binds the owner to his possession, is good in the interest of economic progress. Communism is possible, but only among brothers, in the family, or in a religious and friendly community; it can only be kept up by real love. I don't accept class war; there is difference of class and status; there are degrees among people but that does not mean war: it means the organization of natural inequalities and of those due to historical development, it means a gradual levelling out, progress, and development. I am not so blind and simple as not to see injustice and oppression, and I am aware that individuals, professions, and classes must protect their own interests; but that does not mean *homo homini lupus*, as they used to put it long ago.

While we are on the subject of Marxism I will add this: Marxism is an economic theory and philosophy, particularly a philosophy of history. Economic theory, like every other science, is a matter for scientific investigation, revision, and improvement, and Marxian philosophy, like any other, must be open to criticism and free consideration. That is why revisionism arose, and is called for again. Every revision of a creed or political programme is painful, but without the pain there would be no progress. I have no ready-made Socialist doctrine in my pocket. I would put it like this: I am always on the side of the workmen and working people of all sorts, often for Socialism and occasionally for Marxism.

My opinion of Socialism is derived from my ideas of democracy. Revolution or dictatorship can sometimes abolish bad things, but they never create good and lasting ones. Impatience is fatal in politics. When I consider that all recorded human history goes back only some ten thousand years or so, and that we are still on the threshold of civilization, how can I suppose that some fanatic, either imperialist or revolutionary, will definitely complete our development at one stroke? It is less than two hundred years since serfdom and slavery were abolished, and less than that since forced labour was done away with; about a hundred or even only fifty years since we have worked conscientiously and systematically on the social problems of the workers and the labouring classes generally. We have a hundred thousand, perhaps a million years behind us now: do we consider our civilization complete? Of course the hungry can't satisfy their hunger with thoughts of the future; faith in development and progress doesn't free us from our duties towards the needs of to-day.

* * *

Politically, as I told you, the more radical tendency got the upper hand in the Young Czech Party. But its leaders were still too blind to the needs of the day—the need to organize the nation on a basis of increasing specialization of tendencies and parties.

In contrast to the Young Czech Party I strove to create an organizing tendency—a Party of Organization, I might call it; that was my "realism." Of course it was not understood by the Young Czechs, who opposed it sharply; though nevertheless after their victory of 1891, they accepted us three realists. Of course we couldn't agree for long.

And the movement of the younger generation? That was a kind of synthesis between the Young Czechs and realism; they were young people to whom realism appeared too academic and not national enough.

In 1893 a group of these young people, with Čížek at their head, were tried for high treason. It was a stupid move on the part of the Austrian State, as stupid as the war-time trial of Dr. Rasín and Dr. Kramař. I considered the radicalism of those young people absurd, and could see that, of course, they were not yet fit to take any really serious action. It was in criticism of them that I invented the slogan "Revolution is philistinism." I was very incensed at the murder of the poor cripple, whether he was really in the pay of the police or only believed to be so. But I defended them in the Young Czech Party, though the Party itself disowned them.

Čížek was the leader of the "Younger Generation"; he was a sensible fellow on the staff of the *National News*. The one of the accused whom I knew best was Stanislav Sokol. His father was a teacher, Young Czech Party member, a very good fellow who preached in the style of Comenius. He lived opposite us in Školská Street. The daughter of a Slovak poet, Vera Hurbanová, was living with us—that was all part of my contact with Slovakia. She made friends with the Sokols and went to see them, and through her our two families became acquainted. I remembered that I had known of Stanislav Sokol as a student in our faculty; he was brought up before the faculty for something—a handsome boy with a pale and absolutely transparent-looking face. I took his part against my colleagues. In the case against the "Younger Generation" I did not agree with the way the defence was managed. It was through that that I came to incur the wrath of Dr. Rasín, Čížek's comrade and fellow-victim. I appreciated his matter-of-factness, and I saw nothing to object to even in his brusque manner. I sent books to him and his companions in prison, chiefly Russian literature.

The "Younger Generation" organized themselves in the Radical Progressive Party. Horínek, the brother-in-law of my friend the poet Machar, edited their paper *Progressive News*, together with a little group of other progressives. I had arguments with them at Horínek's house, but we did not understand each other. Stanislav Sokol published a collection of translations from foreign literature chosen by my advice. The first book which he published was Mill's *Subjection of Women*, which my wife translated with the help of her Czech teacher.

Though I did not realize it at the time, I was rather unfair to those young progressives; I did not know that twenty years later I myself should set out on the road of revolution.

* * *

It was a leavening time in literature also. We were being deluged with foreign literature— French writers from Zola to the *Symbolists*, and

Scandinavians as well. The influence of Ibsen began to be felt. Typical of the movement was Machar with his *Confession*. Vilém Mrštík was spreading a knowledge of Russian literature, and I lent him Russian works of criticism which he reviewed. Russian literature, in particular Tolstoi and Dostoyevski had begun to make an impression. It was a sudden flood of new impressions and standards. The University, too, because it was national, exercised considerable influence. Realism stressed the scientific method as an important element of nationalism. In short the 'nineties were a forceful and significant period. Somebody ought to write their history showing how tendencies were progressing and interacting. It was both self-criticism and like the throwing open of windows and doors into the world.

The *Athenaeum* ceased publication, and instead of it I founded *Our Era*. Laichter's new publishing house was disseminating scientific and philosophical books. As for politics, after two years' experience in the Vienna Parliament, I was devoting myself to the study of the development of our Party and of Czech politics since 1848. In the course of these investigations I had a curious experience with the work of Havlíček; I kept finding that he had already written almost everything that I wanted to say politically. In the writings of Palacký I found the reasoned philosophical justification of his political programme, together with his conception of the Czech question, and appreciation of the Czech Reformers, and of the humanitarian ideal. He expresses his philosophy of history most clearly in his pamphlet against Helfert. The agreement between Palacký and Havlíček proved to me the correctness of what I had thought and felt. In politics one must take one's stand on the broader historical issues; one must be in touch not only with one's immediate predecessors, but if possible with all history. And I would add that in politics also the mills of God grind slowly but they grind exceeding small and for all eternity.

* * *

The campaign over the Hilsner affair[1] was a bad business, in which I had to struggle with the superstition about ritual murder. At first I took no interest in the case, but a former student of mine, the Moravian writer Sigmund Münz, came from Vienna to see me and prevailed upon me to take part. I knew the books of the Berlin theologian Starck de-

[1] Hilsner was a young Jew who was accused in 1899 of murdering two girls near the town of Polna and using their blood for rites connected with the Jewish religion. He was tried and convicted, and the trial let loose a storm of anti-semitic feeling. Masaryk was convinced, from a study of the evidence, that Hilsner was innocent, and flung himself into the campaign to prove it.

scribing the origin and history of the ritual superstition. I gave Münz my opinion of the matter, and he
published it in *Neue Freie Presse*. That landed me in
the thick of the fray. The Viennese anti-semites
incited the Czech nationalist and clerical Press to
attack me. Naturally I had to defend myself; having
taken the first step I had to go on. To do this I had
to study criminology and physiology, on both of
which I published detailed articles. I travelled to
Polna to inspect the scene of the crime and its surroundings. And then they said that I had been paid
to do it by the Jews. Students and non-students came
to my University lectures to shout me down. When
they did that I chalked up a protest on the black-
board against the absurd calumny, and challenged
my hearers to come to my house and substantiate it,
giving reasons for their demonstration; one single
student arrived that afternoon to answer my chal-
lenge, a slim, pleasant-faced young man who later
became known as the poet Otakár Theer. So that
my detractors might not imagine that I was afraid
of them, I went the rounds of the whole lecture hall
and challenged each to argument, but none of them
dared. And what do you think? The University,
instead of taking a strong stand and restoring order,
actually suspended my lectures for a fortnight!
That evening the crowd came to my house; I was
in bed with a chill, so my wife went out to them,

188

and told them that I was lying down but that if they wanted to speak to me they could send a deputation. No one came. I suffered much through this campaign, not because I was attacked, but because the level of the attacks was so low. During the war I saw how useful the affair had been to me: the Press of the world is largely managed or financed by Jews; they knew me from the Hilsner case, and repaid me for what I had done for them then by writing favourably about our cause—or at least not unfavourably. That helped us a great deal politically.

*　*　*

Perhaps it is true that I am a born politician; at any rate everything that I was doing at that time, and all my interest, tended, though perhaps indirectly, towards politics. But mere political tactics never satisfied me, whether the question was one of national ideal, social aims, or anything else. I demanded an honest and sensible policy. That was what I meant when I said that even independence would not suffice to save us. I saw in politics only the means; the end for me was a religious and moral one. But I saw that we must be politically free if we were to go freely our own spiritual way. Even to-day I do not suggest that the State is the fulfilment of our cultural mission;

we must prepare for the Kingdom of God that is to come.

Slovakia

I was really brought up half Slovak; my father was a Slovak from Kopčany, and he spoke Slovak till his death. I spoke it too as a child, and I was never conscious of any difference between the Hungarian Slovaks and the Moravian Slovaks among whom I grew up. My grandmother in Kopčany used to bring me a pair of the full white Slovak trousers as a present when she came to see us; I used to wear them at nights to go to bed in, because I was dressed "like a gentleman." My family was in constant touch with Kopčany and Holíč, and at Kopčany I often heard Hungarian spoken; a few Hungarian words would even crop up in our talk at home. One or two young men on my father's side of the family became quite Magyarized; some cousins from Hungary even came to see me in Prague. While in Vienna I examined the traces of the Slovaks who had lived there at different periods, such as the poet Kollár and the writer Kuzmány, who was the first, I believe, to attempt a Slovak novel.

After I was in Prague I went to a meeting of University professors at the Hotel de Saxe; during our discussion I raised the point that we Czechs should work for political union with the Slovaks. A number of my colleagues opposed me and quoted the authority of Rieger, who had said that the Slovak question was *causa finita*; they considered it a matter of historical State rights: the Bohemian State was in law only Bohemia, Moravia, and Silesia —they renounced Slovakia. But I was against their exclusively historical theory, because what, after all, is a historical right in reality? Is right independent of time and of whether or no a claim was realized in practice? Is not a right simply a right, no matter when it was or was not valid? Could not the Austrians and Hungarians answer us with "historical rights"? I have never refused to accept so-called historical right, but I combine it with natural right. In the first place it is more democratic; right is not a hereditary privilege, but the claim of each nation and each individual to its own life. And in the second place I was influenced by the fate of Slovakia; in conceding our historical right of the State we should have had to leave Slovakia to the Hungarians. And lastly I disliked the idea of "historical" right as a notion engendered by reactionary, pre-Revolutionary Germany. The young Czechs in their beginnings were quite justified in claiming natural right side by side with historical right. We had a certain number of Slovakophiles who were conscious of natural unity, of brotherhood, but it was more a matter of literature than politics; they did not dare to carry it to its political conclusion. The spirit of Kollár was apparent in all this, who had been satisfied with racial and cultural independence; of political independence he and his contemporaries never so much as dreamed.

I was particularly anxious that the Czechs and the people of Prague should really know Slovakia: to sing Slovak songs was not enough for me. So when we founded *Time* I took care that we should have a section entirely devoted to Slovakia. I also invited Slovak students from the University to see me. As early as the end of the 'eighties I had founded a regular summer school at Bystrička near Turčanský Svatý Martin, with the deliberate object of getting to know the Slovaks at close quarters, and even influencing them. For more than ten years I went and stayed there at intervals.

In those days even Hurban-Vajanský was a Czechophile; it was only later that he succumbed to fantastic Russophilism, and looked to Russia for the redemption of the Slovaks. I was on friendly terms with him, and he and many other friends, including Věšín, who might almost be described as the official painter of the Slovaks, found their way to Svatý Martin. I went to Mošovce and spoke on Kollár on the spot where the house had stood in which he was born, and the Hungarian police wanted to arrest me for it.

At the end of the 1890's there was a meeting of Slovaks at Svatý Martin; the opposition, made up of the younger wing, came to see me at Bystrička. With them I discussed a Slovak programme of cultural and political work. The result of this was the foundation in 1898 of the review *The Voice*; it was chiefly supported by a small group, including Makovický, who became Tolstoi's doctor, and a little apart from them stood Hodža:[1] these were opposed by Vajanský, who later lost himself in Russophilism, by the Catholics with Hlinka[2] at their head, and even by the Protestants headed by Janoš. A more intense life was beginning. One Slovak organization after another was founded.

When I wanted to go abroad in 1914 I already counted absolutely on Slovakia. But in order to have full power to act in the direction that I wished to take, I wanted to know what the other members of Parliament said about it, and I sounded them. I talked to Antonín Hajn as a legal authority; he grasped my point immediately, and told me that

[1] Later Minister of Education in the Czechoslovak Republic.

[2] Father Hlinka was a Slovak nationalist leader under the Hungarian régime and later one of the leaders of the Clerical Party in the Czechosloval Parliament.

he knew an officer on the General Staff who could draw us a map of the future Slovakia based on national and strategic frontiers. And he did actually bring me a map on which the future frontier was sketched in pencil; our present frontiers are almost identical with those on that map.

And after I had gone abroad I was glad that the Slovak Štefánik had begun the same work as ourselves with the same aim.

*　　*　　*

When the folk at Bystrička told me that there were bears roaming the mountains and that they came down to the fields after the oats, I didn't believe it. I thought that the shepherds themselves sometimes killed or sold a sheep and then put the blame on the bear. Our neighbour Markovický once took me to see what a bear can do. He sits down on his hind quarters in a field of oats and crushes the oats into his mouth with his forepaws— so; then he moves on, still squatting, till he has squatted over the whole field; when he has finished the field looks as if it had been trampled down. Markovický showed me one of these fields. "All right," I thought, "if we have bears, let's hunt them." My friends lent me an enormous gun, a muzzle-loader, which must have been handed down from the Turkish army, and we went one evening at full moon to lie in wait for him, Markovický, the forester, and I. We waited near the field of oats in a clearing on the edge of the forest for an hour, and then another, and still the bear didn't come. It was nearly midnight, the stars were shining, and on the bare hills all around the shepherds were lighting bonfires, there and over yonder. A beautiful sight it was. We forgot the bear and began talking, Markovický smoked, the forester went to sleep. And suddenly I saw the bear come out of the forest into the clearing, about thirty or thirty-five paces away. He was a gigantic, lovely beast. I picked up my gun but I couldn't shoot, I was trembling like a leaf. In the meantime the bear had got wind of us; he sprang into the oats and from there into the forest. And then I behaved shamefully. I was not afraid but rather astonished that there should be such things as bears, in which I had never really believed, or perhaps just excited by the sight of such a strong and beautiful beast and the idea that I should shoot it seemed to me treachery!

The second time I got a bear, after having lain in wait in the forest. He was a smaller one this time; I shot him in the chest; he ran on a little way and then fell down, but he was still alive. So we sat down and waited; he lived for as long as our dog still kept barking at him. When the dog stopped barking we went to fetch the dead bear. I still have his skin somewhere at home.

The third time that I met a bear it happened like this. I was leaving Bystrička for Prague, so I went out alone to say farewell to the mountains. I had a gun and a dog, a brave little fellow. I went along the path in the mountains, and there I saw a bear about two hundred yards away, another, a gigantic beast, eating bilberries. I drew nearer to him against the wind so that he didn't scent me. But my dog hurried on in front of me; the bear sniffed him and went for him. The bear raised his head so that I had to shoot quickly at about a hundred and twenty paces. He got a wound in the chest and rolled over, but he picked himself up and ran into the forest. I went after him. Of course one must not chase a wounded bear, but I forgot that. I forgot everything except that I must get him! He was bleeding and he fled further and further into the mountains; I chased him a long way but I did not get him, and it was getting dark. Early next morning we went out after him; we followed his tracks to the boundary of the next estate, further than that we couldn't go. They wrote to me that they found him on the third day on that estate, all eaten up by worms already. Folk say that bears are like the people in the part of the country where they live; our bears in Slovakia are good-natured.

I have shot wild boars too, but not other animals, though I have always enjoyed fishing for trout and grayling; it was not so much the fishing that I liked as the wading in the water and the lovely hours on the banks of the stream. Wherever there are trout it is always beautiful. I taught the folk of Svatý Martin to catch fish with fly instead of worms; worms are ugly, and you have to sit with them in the same place, while with fly you can walk about. It isn't only that; you have to choose your artificial fly carefully according to the flies in season; you must throw your fly on its line to the fish; when he bites you must pull him in quickly, and carefully wind in your line on the reel, and catch him from below in your net. There is an art in all that. Usually I put back my fishes into the water.

Later I gave it all up; my wife was so sorry for the beasts and fishes.

* * *

When I am in the country I notice how decisive childhood's impressions are for one's whole life. I was born in the plains, and to this day I do not care for mountains and forests; they oppress me somehow. Give me the plains, the sea, or the steppes, or, if there are hills, then let me be on the top and look down. In the plains you have the most beautiful sunsets; I have seen some such marvellous ones that they have remained with me all my life; one was in New Jersey and another at Olomouc. Once I saw Prague Castle from Štefaník Bridge in the mist at twilight—an exquisite picture; another time, standing on Legii Bridge I saw the silver morning light streaming up from under Palacký Bridge. Pictures like this I can't forget. Once I was travelling by train in winter; as we came out of a tunnel I caught sight of a tree which still had its leaves; it was sheltered by the embankment of the tunnel. It was only a glimpse, but it swept over me like a miracle. In that moment I understood pantheism—the deification of nature. I understood it, but I have never accepted it.

I like the country better than town. My four years abroad were all the harder for me because I had always to live in great cities. I noticed on my return, after the war, that I had grown to love the country even more. Perhaps some day better improved communication will make possible the de-urbanization which the Socialists have in their programme; then even the factories will not be crowded together in towns, and the towns will be healthier—so that even civilization is bringing folk nearer to nature.

I do not see things as you do; I do not look for

individuality in nature, I rather look at the whole, the colours and form of the landscape; I love the sun, the fresh breeze and the wind, the freedom. You say that I am always looking into the distance, and it is so. I scarcely notice my immediate surroundings; even to-day I couldn't tell you how my house at Topolčanky is furnished. But I know all the mountains on the horizon; I have ridden up them on my old horse, Hector, up to the very top, to see what lies on the other side.

Every time I look at a flower, an insect, a bird, I want to know all about it, what, how, and why it is like that; but I have not the time for it. I have too much to do with people; they are part of my business. So that is my link with nature; I am happy when I am surrounded by nature—but I still think of people!

The Years 1900 to 1910

You ask what I was doing from my fiftieth to my sixtieth year. . . . Well, really nothing. . . . At least I had more peace; those ugly conflicts were behind me. There was the campaign for the eight-hour working day; there was the agitation for universal suffrage—of course I joined in movements like that. I had my lectures at the University; I have forgotten now what I lectured about. In the course of them I touched on our social conditions, in particular in the lectures on practical philosophy. I had my lecture-room full, although I was not a good teacher. I held public meetings and extension lectures, public debates, and so on.

It may be a weakness of mine, but I am shy of people. I don't like speaking in public; whenever I have had to give a lecture or make a speech at a public meeting or in the University, I have always felt nervous; and yet how many speeches I have had to make! I get that feeling of fright even to-day when I have to appear or speak in public. When it is simply a case of speaking for the sake of speaking—art for art's sake—the art of the orator—it is easy. But to speak on practical matters, on things which ought to be done, is a very different thing. I have never liked taking a front place in the full view of the public; second or third place is quite enough for me. Certainly I have never pushed myself into public activities. I have always made excuses when other people wanted to push me into them. But even when I did it unwillingly with the feeling that I was wasting my time, there was always some logic in it, and it led to something. That has been the case in everything.

Early one morning in about the year 1902 an American came to see me with an introduction from Louis Léger in Paris. Before he told me what

he wanted I thought that he must be some journalist
in need of help, and I was calculating in my head
how much I could manage to give him. But it
turned out that he was Mr. Crane, a Chicago manufacturer. He had a business house in Russia too,
and had been there and become interested in Slav
questions. He had founded a fund for Slavonic
studies at Chicago University, and came to invite
me to lecture there! I delivered a course of ten
or twenty lectures in Chicago, on Dostoyevski,
Kiryeyevski, and our own problems; and besides
that I travelled about and spoke to our fellow
countrymen over there. Crane was an acquaintance
of Professor Wilson, and his son was War Minister
during Wilson's presidency, and helped us a great
deal during the war. In 1907 I went to America
again, during the Boston Congress of free religious
workers, and lectured there. I lectured to Czech
gatherings, too, on that visit, in particular to the
Society of Freethinkers in Chicago, who published
some of my lectures in book form.

I went once or twice to England too, during
these years. While I was at the Anti-Alcoholic
Congress in Vienna I made an extempore speech
which some English people there liked, so that I
got to know a number of professors and journalists.
Later I went to England with my daughter Alice,
and we visited Elizabeth Blackwell, a remarkable

woman who opened the way for women in the medical profession. So when I was in England during the war I found that I had quite a number of friends.

*   *   *

It is not true that I founded the Progressive or, as it was called, the Realistic Party; on the contrary, I was against its foundation. I should have preferred to influence public opinion through the Press alone, or else to develop a kind of Fabian movement among us, which would have worked in all parties by means of lectures and debates. But the young men decided to found a party, because there was no room for them in the other parties; and when they had got together and invited me to join them, I did. That was in 1900. At its first meetings the party drew up its whole programme in a document called *The Red Book*. The Realists were really not a mere political party, they did not only deal with current politics; they brought a tendency, a critical and scientific tendency, into our public life, strengthening our politicians and making them more scientific and also more world-wide in their outlook—drawing them into "non-political politics" as I sometimes called them.

I was twice in a political party, in the Young Czechs as a Realist, and in the Realistic Party. I am not a party man. It is not that I don't admit the necessity of parties. But I always strove for the reform of those already existing. To a certain extent I was successful, but with many conflicts thrust on me by the conditions prevailing. I came to Prague a stranger, and a stranger I remained for a long time; that to a certain extent explains my peculiar position.

The Czechs had only one party at first, the nameless party of Palacký and Havlíček, but a split began when a new element entered, that of the advocates of rural interests. At the time when the Young Czech Party was formed the country towns were awaking from their provincial dream; new men came crowding on to the scene, with their sleeves rolled up for action. There you get the radical tendency of the Young Czechs.

Socialism was the gift of industrialization, the crowding together of workmen, men with the same clothes and the same needs, under one roof in the same factory. Socialism developed everywhere, in Germany, France, England, Russia. The Young Czechs did not understand this, and they struck a blow at themselves in attacking the Socialists.

Besides the workman we had the farmer, an individualist in economic affairs, and a conservative.

If you add the Catholics you get four parties altogether, the two big parties of the Socialists and Agrarians, and against them the Bourgeois Party, as it was called, and the Catholic Party.

But the specialization or, if you like, the disintegration, was going on, and small parties were beginning to be formed.

A party system in politics is natural, but it has its good and its bad side, like everything human. Anything can be abused; it all depends on whether folk are decent and well educated. I personally have more faith in people than in institutions; that is to say, political parties. It is certainly an interesting problem why we should have so many parties when the English and Americans manage with only two or three; but the situation is not specifically Czech; the German parties in Czechoslovakia are just as divided. In both cases the origin of the splitting up was really in Vienna; Vienna governed and administered; Parliament and the Diets were under Government control and the Crown; so the parties did not bear the burden of responsibility, and it was nothing to the Government when they split. This training which we received under Austria is not overcome yet; we demand de-Austrianization, but we are really still living under the old régime. The fact that the smaller parties united after the Revolution and formed the National Democrats was good theoretically, and a step in the right direction; so is the present tendency to consider the formation of larger blocks; all this shows a greater sense of statesmanship. Statesmen are those men active in politics and public affairs who really bear in mind the interest of the State in whatever they do; to men such as these politics only means harmonizing and organizing smaller bodies into one larger whole, uniting all efforts; this is a policy which goes beyond the frontiers of the State, and it is what our post-war era needs.

*　*　*

Newspapers, the literary organ of politics, have interested me all my life. To-day I should probably be a journalist if I hadn't another job. In about 1876, while I was still a student, I was writing to the newspapers under the initial "Y"; nine or ten years later in Prague I arranged with Dr. Julius Grégr that I should edit the scientific section in his paper *National News*; I even wrote an article for the German paper *Politik* about that time— I think the subject was *Mehr Gewerbebildung*; I don't really remember what reason I had for wanting to write in a German paper; perhaps I was simply invited to by someone. Dr. Grégr made a fuss about it; he considered it a breach of my

205

contract with his paper, an idea that had never for a moment occurred to me. This incident certainly served later to aggravate the trouble about the manuscripts. When our group of "Realists" was negotiating about union with the Old Czechs, our main interest was the party newspapers; we wanted to improve them and influence them; of course the journalists among the Old Czechs were dead against us. Then in 1887 there was that unfortunate business over the new review, *Time*. It was founded by the younger members of our group who wanted a paper of their own; I knew nothing about it till I received the first copy with the article by Schauer which was attributed to me and caused such a stir; then I answered the charges in *Time*, and from that time onward became a contributor. Later I wrote in *Our Era*.

In 1900, thirteen years after its foundation, *Time* began to come out as a daily; from then onwards I was a regular member of the staff, and did more advising than writing myself. My pleasantest memory of the co-operative work there is of the period at the beginning of the war; we used to meet, Dr. Herben, Pfeffermann, Kunte, myself, and later Beneš, and study the situation of the belligerents carefully; good articles resulted from our discussions, in so far as the censor of those days let them appear. I wrote two articles for *Our*

Era in which I estimated the strength of the two opposing camps.

I was afraid that if the war were short it would not liberate us, even though Austria were defeated. We were not prepared, and the belligerent Powers scarcely knew anything about us. So I pondered and speculated how long it could last. Though I did not want it to be short, I could not help reproaching myself with cruelty for wishing it long.

There is so much that I should like to say about newspapers. I am angry with them every day, which only proves to me how much I care for them. We Czechs have had two great journalists: Havlíček and Neruda.[1] Neruda, of course, was only a journalist indirectly, in his essays and sketches and critical notes. But they show all the essentials of a good journalist. He must be well-informed and capable, able to observe and appraise; he must be indifferent to nothing, since the whole world, the whole of contemporary life is his canvas. To be a journalist means to observe and understand the contemporary world. I say observe and understand since the journalist who estimates everything from his paper's standpoint and cuts his coat according to

[1] Jan Neruda (1834–1891) was a journalist and poet of democratic views. He wrote chiefly essays and sketches which were published in *National News*; best known among them are the "Tales from Malá Strána," describing the familiar figures of the part of Prague where he lived.

the blessed cloth of party politics either preaches or quarrels, and that is all. The mere local reporter who describes events accurately is doing better, more honest work. Of course a good journalist must have character; he must defend freedom of speech—freedom, freedom! . . .

* * *

In the years 1905 and 1906 there arose the question of universal suffrage; the Emperor and Taaffe hoped and expected that the entry of the Socialist parties into Parliament would be weakened by nationalist divisions; the Czech parties also were in favour of it, because it was our only method of gaining votes. In 1907 the first elections were held under general suffrage. In Valašsko in Moravia there was a progressive political association and also some of my own disciples; I don't know who first suggested my name, but when the writ for elections was issued they proposed me as a candidate. That was how I came to stand for Valašsko, and I also got to know that this division had the largest number of subscribers to *Our Era*. My opponent was the candidate of the Clerical Party, Povondra, supported mainly by the clergy. They canvassed against me among the poor Valachs by telling them that I wanted to destroy the family. There was, as a matter of fact, an agitation at the time for the

208

introduction of legal divorce, but I had no con-
nexion with it; it was my clercial opponents who
ascribed the agitation to me. I used to go to my
election meetings with a Bible in my pocket; when
some priest or parson defended the indissolubility
of marriage I would read aloud from the Gospel
of St. Matthew a passage proving that Jesus
admits divorce; and then it would be all up with
the reverend gentleman. I was disgusted with the
way political speakers only repeated party catch-
words at their meetings; I preferred to speak on
alcoholism or economic affairs or something like
that, so that the audience should have something of
lasting interest. Well, the long and the short of it was
that I won the election and went back to Vienna
again. There were two of us Realists elected, Professor Drtina and I.

Why did the Clerical Party oppose me? When I
first came to Prague as a professor I was received
fairly well, even by the Catholics. Father Vychodil[1]
wrote appreciatively of my paper on Blaise Pascal.
But later they ferreted out a remark of mine, in my
thesis on Suicide, to the effect that for us Czechs
Catholicism is an impossible doctrine; that did not
worry the Catholics in Germany proper, who

[1] Lecturer in Theology in Brünn and later director of the Brünn
University library. He was a Benedictine, a philosopher of note,
and an authority on Aristotle.

criticized the work very favourably. But German Catholics were always more cultured. I believe I criticized the philosophical works of the Czech Catholics in the *Athenaeum*. They were weak. Later, during the manuscript controversy, it was the Catholic daily, *The Czech*, which attacked me most bitterly; and during the Hilsner affair[1] it was again the Clerical newspapers which took the prize. They it was who started the story that I depraved the young, etc. Of course they could not forgive me for basing my philosophy on the Czech Reformation, and for putting our native Czech culture in the place of a fictitious ancient Slav culture. The point of departure both of my philosophy and policy is the Czech Reformation, because, for me, it was above all a moral and religious movement, not a theological one. The starting-point of Huss and of Štítný after him was the reformation of morals; I found mention in their works of the thing that had worried me as a child, when I observed the strange life of the priest. My quarrel with the Church was also a matter of morals, not of dogma. The Protestants have, after all, the same fundamental dogmas as the Catholics. But I had to reject dogmas because they could not stand before the criticism of my reason; that applies to the dogmas of all denominations. What I cannot

[1] See p. 187.

accept by reason, I cannot accept even by faith.
Perhaps some day I shall publish my final opinion
on these problems.

Further I did not then and still do not love
liberalism in so far as it implies religious indifference and superficiality. Catholicism with its mistakes—especially in Austria, where it was the
official faith, protected by the police and guarded
by all the offices of State—only fostered this liberal
laxity. I always said that Jesus had no need of the
police. Of course in Austria the struggle against
the State was also a struggle against the State
Church. Really it was owing to this alliance of
sword and altar that the religious life among our
people became so weak. Our Reformation was
fundamentally a movement against Austria—that
is why our liberals have never fully understood it.

In the course of my fight with the clergy I had
a public debate at Hradec Králové with Father
Reyl and Father Jemelka.[1] It was a sign of progress that such a discussion was possible. I had
a large following of young students and priests,
anxious for me to advise them whether or not to
leave the Church, since they had such and such
scruples. As a rule I advised against such a step,
for I saw that their doubts were not strong enough to

[1] Two priests very active in polemics in Hradec Králové. Father
Reyl is now a member of the Czechoslovak Senate.

lead them to another positive faith. One young
chaplain confessed to me that the only thing which
interested him in the exercise of his office was to
watch the women and girls. I did not advocate
leaving the Church so long as the cause was only
indifference, or a political impetus like the "*Los
von Rom*" movement, or the desire to marry; I
wanted people to be honest in their religious
feelings.

* * *

While we are on the subject of the Church, I
would add that neither Church nor theology means
religion to me; that is to say, they are not the whole of
religion. We intellectuals easily grasp the teaching,
the theory of this Church or that. But that does
not imply religious life. I cannot consider religion
in the abstract. I can see even to-day a Sunday
morning at Čejkovice: the whole village comes
together, acquaintances greet each other, boys and
girls pass in couples, all dressed in their Sunday
best; the scent of incense rises, music plays, the
whole village sings, they all stand up together, kneel
down together, squire and groom; you have the
whole drama at the altar; you have the sermon
which you can understand and the mysterious Latin
which you cannot. Think what a Sunday like that
gives to a man, and how it makes him at one with

his fellows! The Catholic Mass is, as it were, a popular festival; Protestantism, with its less ceremonious rites, penetrates more into everyday life. The Church as a whole shows its influence in that the whole year is linked and divided by religious festivals: Sundays and holidays—natural holidays, and holidays which have come down from pagan days. The Church presides over a man's whole life, his birth, coming of age, marriage, and death; it is all ordained and systematized to the highest degree. You must remember that the folk in a small village had nothing else; that made it a very strong bond. The rites of the Church—like other festivals—were evolved in times when folk could not read as they do to-day, when they were an unlettered mass; and this state lasted till the nineteenth century! To-day they read, they have theatres, concerts, and lectures, they have cinema and wireless for eyes and ears; they have clubs, sports, and political parties to draw them together. In the place of divine service they have a fat Sunday paper; when I glance at it I often ask myself: Is that all we have to replace the divine service which I knew in my childhood?

Of course the progress of history itself alters the mission of the Church. The Church really took over the Roman Empire and preserved part of the culture of antiquity; for a thousand years it had the monopoly of schools and culture; the whole of humanitarian activities were reserved to it, hospitals and the care of the poor; among a hurly-burly of nations and potentates it maintained not merely Pan-Europe but the unity of the world; its missions founded the movements by which the world was civilized. All this meant an immense international, universal programme of organization. To-day these tasks have been entrusted to other hands, those of the State. The Church no longer maintains all the schools; she has ceased to foster and control learning; even the humanitarian services have been taken over by the State and its social legislation; international and cultural relations have passed into lay hands; economic interest links the world, whether for good or ill. If I express it by the formula that theocracy is giving way to democracy that does not mean that religion is losing its importance and its mission. The care of the soul, the practical care for morals, is still in the hands of the Church. If the priests attended to this—they would be the nearest to Jesus. In almost every family you find some moral problem; to perceive this trouble and fortify the soul which is sinking beneath it should be the duty of the priest. But to do this the priest needs knowledge of men and deep inner experience—and where are we to find men like that?

This development cannot be stopped; the world

214

has step by step become more of a united whole, more organized in States; the Church has ceased to be a political and social force. And besides that, more criticism and science are slowly breaking down all dogmas and theologies. Hence the religious crisis in all the Churches.

The task of Christianity—the task of the Church —is as great, nay even greater, than it was two thousand years ago: its task is to become the real herald of active love and builder of the soul. How that is to be accomplished the Churches themselves must say; the Church to-day and to-morrow will be more individual; it will answer the personal spiritual needs of people—I am not a prophet, but I think I am one of those future believers. We need freedom of science and research, intellectual integrity in matters of religion, we need tolerance too, but not spiritual indifference; no, what we need is faith, living faith in something higher than ourselves something great, sublime, eternal.

My quarrel with the historians? Well, it was like this. I am also a philosopher of history. While I was still at school I puzzled my head and wondered whether schoolboys a million years hence would still have to recite the dates of the kings of France, and the other potentates, and their wars. That isn't history; it is only the history of something; you can have the history of mathematics, philosophy, art; you can have the history of hats or boots if you like, or the history of the whole of education or of the whole universe. Always it is something which changes and develops; it is not a movement in itself, it is something which moves. Now I should like the historians to tell me what this thing is, of which they are so busy writing the history? If it is the history of the State, then let them tell us what the State is, and how the State of to-day grew out of its beginnings in the past.

I am not against history but I am against historicism; by that I mean that the past is not a decisive argument in itself, because in the past there is both good and bad. I base myself only on what is good in the past. In the same way the present is not an argument in itself, nor is our—so much invoked—modernity. Both oppressor and oppressed can base their claim on historical rights. What has been and the fact that it has been is a comfortable argument for the reactionary; what interests me is how the good and the bad which were yesterday, and are to-day, have originated. History is the teacher of life, but of all the historians we have had, how many have been real teachers?

* * *

The Zagreb case and the Friedjung case which followed it were a training in diplomacy for me;

through them I came to join in a campaign against Aehrenthal, the Austro-Hungarian Minister for Foreign Affairs, and to be active in foreign politics. It happened in this way. In 1909 fifty-three Croat intellectuals and peasants came up for trial on a charge of high treason. The Hungarian police had forged the documents on which the accusation was based. It was a hanging matter. Now I had acquaintances in Bosnia and Croatia dating from the time of my campaign against Kállay, and also a number of pupils. They came to me and begged me to come to Zagreb. I wasn't at all keen to go. I was afraid it would take up a lot of my time. However, in the end to Zagreb I went. I was present at the trial, and afterwards I brought up the whole case in Parliament. The sentence was reversed.

The second instance was the case of the Viennese historian, Friedjung. He published a forged document which was to prove a Serbian plot against Austria. I could see at the first glance that the thing was a forgery; for as I had experience of the people in Serbia and Croatia I knew what their intentions were and what they were really trying to do. The Croatian deputy, Supilo, came to see me and assured me that he had proofs that behind the forgeries were the deputy Forgach and agents of the Minister for Foreign Affairs. That was not enough for me; I wanted to have all the details and to verify them

217

there and then. So I went to Belgrade several times; there I even found the little holes in the doors on which the document had been pinned when they photographed it. I even went to see Vasić, who had prepared the document. Since that time I have had friends in Serbia and Croatia, and I worked with them also during the war. In the case of these affairs I also came into touch with Mr. Wickham Steed, the *Times* correspondent in Vienna for the Balkans and Central Europe. This opened the columns of *The Times* to us during the war.

*   *   *

In 1910, when I had my sixtieth birthday, there was a dinner and there were speeches. They say that in replying to the speeches I said that all that I had done so far was mere preparation, and that my real work was still before me. Afterwards people interpreted that as a prophecy of what I was to do during the war. That's all nonsense. I didn't know how to answer all the speeches—and I could feel that I had not yet come to the end of my work.

Before the War

In the years immediately before the war I was in Parliament. At the same time I wrote and published my book *Russia and Europe.* Then the German publisher, Diederichs, read my obituary notice on Tolstoi; I made an agreement with him that I would collect my studies on Russia and let him publish them. Two volumes have now been published; the third, on Dostoyevsky, I still have in manuscript. I should like to write on all kinds of other subjects—but the time! Where am I to get the time from?

I was elected to Parliament in 1911. Professor Drtina had ceased to be a member, so that I was the only Realist. I used to forgather with the two members of the Constitutional Party and the two Moravian Progressives.

Then there was the Šviha affair. It showed that we were not prepared for what was before us. Fancy charging a Czech Member of Parliament with being paid by the police like an ordinary spy —think what their opinion must have been of us! I was convinced that Šviha was not identical with the police spy Wiener; it is true that he was used for political ends by the heir to the throne, whom he furnished with information which he had picked up in his capacity of Member of Parliament; he was in debt, and the heir to the throne offered to pay him for his services, but because he was a skinflint he had the money given to Šviha by the police. At least that was how it appeared to me at the time.

Politically it was a greater crime than if Švíha had been paid by the police; but from a human point of view it was more tolerable. I went into the case thoroughly; I wanted Švíha to be tried *in camera caritatis*, as had been done in other cases. I could not foresee at that time that my part in the Švíha case would annoy certain people to such an extent that they did not get over it even with the outbreak of the world war.

But on the other hand it is true, and I willingly admit it, that in this and other cases I made mistakes. And certainly I was made to pay for them to the full.

*   *   *

Strange that in the course of my life I have so often become involved in all sorts of problems and disputes, often even against my will; I used sometimes to think that I was wasting my time with so many different interests. It was only during the war that I realized that everything, or almost everything, that I had done at one time and another —and even the things that had been thrust upon me—had been useful in some way. It was a good thing, and one that stood me in good stead during the war, that I had been born half Slovak, that I had lived among Slovaks, and worked with them; I was able to talk to them, speak on their behalf like one of themselves.

THE MIDDLE YEARS

It was also good that I had studied in Vienna and was known there. As a Member of Parliament I had carefully observed the court at Vienna, the military bigwigs, the nobility, and the higher bureaucracy; all this knowledge came in useful during the war, when I was showing up the moral disintegration and the inevitable downfall of Austria.

My conflicts and disputes, whether about manuscripts, constitutional rights, or the meaning of our history, led me not only into politics but to the study of our national questions; I could not have gone into politics if I had not been forced to take such an active part in the political problems of our nation. In the course of my various battles I came to know all about our people, and I also learnt diplomacy—for there is a literary and journalistic diplomacy—and all this I needed, and was able to use, during the war.

Ever since my childhood Slav problems have filled my head: the Polish question and later the Russian problems. All that I had read and thought about Russia brought me into contact with Russians and gave me a good deal of weight among them; I learnt what we can, and what we cannot, expect of Russia; I got to learn the methods which I used later in forming our revolutionary army. If I had not known Russia so well I should perhaps have failed to find my bearings in the chaos of the Russian Revolution. I was on friendly terms with the Poles; as a Member of Parliament, I had the opportunity to champion the cause of the Jugoslavs in Bosnia, in the Zagreb case, and the Friedjung affair. That won us the co-operation of the Jugoslavs during the war. During the Friedjung affair I had to do a piece of detective work, and in the war that experience was valuable. My quarrel with Aehrenthal initiated me in official diplomacy, and brought me into contact with Wickham Steed and Seton Watson. It also made me known in England and France and elsewhere.

My wife was an American; that opened the Anglo-Saxon world to me. The knowledge of its language and culture made my work in England and America possible during the war. My knowledge of languages has been very useful to me everywhere; I have been able to talk and lecture in Russia, France, England, and America. I could even get on somehow in Italian. Through my lectures in America I made friends with people who were of great service to us in the war.

It was only in the war that I came to realize the worth of the Hilsner case. In all the Allied countries the Jews had great influence in the newspaper world; wherever I went the papers wrote in our favour, or at least not against us. You cannot imagine how much that meant for our cause.

THE MIDDLE YEARS

I have had other experiences like these. I believe in the doctrine of final causes, I believe that each one of us is led by Providence—but how? That I cannot say.

* * *

I am a Realist, as we said, but I like romance. I see no contradiction in that. The romantic poets were nearest to me personally: Mácha, Pushkin, de Musset, Byron.

I continually have to hold myself in check; when I chose realism and scientific method it meant that I had to control my own romanticism, and to practise mental discipline. I force myself to be a realist in practice: I force myself continuously and consciously. In the same way I overcame the Slav anarchy in myself, in philosophy and other things, by the help of the teachers of the English-speaking world; Locke, Hume, and the other empiricists mitigated the teaching of Plato in me. People seem not to understand that criticism, especially bitter criticism, is often a sign of self-criticism, a painful confession. And I always have within me the conflict between the impulsive Slovak and the sober Czech. Man is not a simple being; it has been my misfortune that not only my adversaries but my followers even wanted to make me a one-sided type.

Take, for instance, my notorious rationalism. Of course, as long as I want to teach and demonstrate I must maintain reason and reasonable arguments. But always and everywhere, in science and in politics, my motive force was an ethical one—and ethics I base on feeling, on love, on sympathy, on humanity. Circumstances often helped me to criticize right and left; but my criticism did not spring from rationalism, certainly not from rationalism alone. Logic and feeling do not exclude each other.

Politics contain an element of poetry, in fact they have as much poetry in them as they have creative force. I think that we can consciously form and fashion our own lives and those of the people near us to a considerable extent: life can and must create; life itself is drama, just as Shakespearean drama is life. And what are politics in the best sense of the word but the conscious forming of people, the fashioning and transforming of real life?

Politics, too, demand a balance between reason and feeling. Even in the most delicate political situation we must notice and plan carefully, what, how, and on whom we can count; it has to be as accurate as mathematics; our feelings must never err in their observations and calculations. But the aim, the ideal, is not laid down by reason alone, but by feeling also. The means are dictated by reason; but we can change the situation to suit our aim, we can introduce new elements into it, something of our own. That is creation; that is the poetry of life.

The most romantic time of my life, of course, was during the war years, though even then I worked by rule and calculation. I am not thinking only of the romance of conspiracy and war. When I think how we went into it unprepared, and yet really completing a century of the efforts of such men as Dobrovsky, Kollár, Palacký, and Havlíček; how isolated we were, we abroad and those at home, and yet with what sureness we fulfilled the mandate of the whole nation; how we set out with naked hands, and how at the end we returned bearing them freedom, the Republic, Slovakia, Ruthenia—it still seems like a dream to me. There you have an example of Providence.

You see how it is: the method must be absolutely practical, reasonable, realistic—but the aim, the whole, the conception is an eternal poem. Goethe has a nice phrase: *Exakte Phantasie.*

* * *

The romance of life! Sometimes long, long ago, I thought I should like to write a Czech novel and to crowd into it the novel of my life. I began it once, while I was at school, and again a couple of times after that, but only really seriously after my

225

experiences in Prague. It was to be a piece of auto-biography, a *Dichtung und Wahrheit*, but I didn't manage to do it properly; I gave it up and burnt what I had written. I realized that I have not the artistic skill, and I did not want to preach a professorial sermon. My life has been full, packed with events; I forget the details now, and the exact chronological sequence. I have method even in my way of forgetting; everything that is finished with I throw out of my head, so as to have it free and tidy, just as one clears out a writing desk. And to be quite honest, I cannot tell everything, not only out of consideration for others. I doubt whether one has words adequate to express the innermost things. Anyone who understands how to read will find me between the lines of my books.

THE WAR AND AFTER

THE WAR AND AFTER

The First Part of the War

THE outbreak of the war found me in Saxony on a holiday. When the heir to the Austrian throne was shot in Serajevo I had both expected and not expected that things would not end there. I expected something because for years I had felt something in the air; I expected nothing because I knew that the Serbian Government had had no hand in the outrage. I knew plenty of people in the south, and knew their plans. There was certainly agitation against Austria-Hungary in Bosnia and Herzagovina; there was agitation in Croatia; but the Serbian Government was not involved. It wanted to come to an understanding with Austria, and Pashich, through me, had made the Minister Berchtold quite decent proposals. On the Serbian side there was goodwill. And I also know how moderate official Serbia was after the war.

When the order for mobilization was given, I couldn't get back from Germany; there were no trains. So I watched the mobilization, even going to Dresden and other towns for that purpose, and I could not help being impressed. Such seriousness, order, and such preparedness "to the last button."

During the whole mobilization I never saw a single drunken German, though whole trainloads of Austrian levies on their way back to report for duty were dead drunk. I know that they drank to drown despair, but that too reflects on the State.

I hoped that Germany would be beaten, but I saw that it would be an enormous task, more difficult than anyone believed; Austria, on the other hand, would soon be at the end of her strength, especially her moral strength. I feared for France; I thought she would very likely be surprised by a swift German onrush, and perhaps her very existence threatened. It was Russia that I was most doubtful about. My last visit had been in 1910, when my purpose was more to see the Russian Army than to see Tolstoi. I had noticed then the lack of preparation and the disorder. The Russo-Japanese War had improved things a little, but not much. I was acquainted in Vienna with Svatkovsky, the representative of the Russian Official Telegraph Agency for Austria-Hungary and the Balkans; he visited me, whether at the beginning of the war or shortly after the Serajevo murder I cannot remember; he spoke about Russia with much apprehension, and did not agree with the plan current at the time of giving Bohemia to some Russian Grand Duke. He said to me: "In Prague you would not put up for a fortnight with the rule of the best of Russian Grand

Dukes." I did not expect much of Tsarist Russia either militarily or morally. My belief that Germany would lose the war was based rather on calculations and comparisons of the resources of both sides in men and raw material. That America might help did not occur to me.

When I got back to Prague I tried to perceive in what spirit the Czechs were reporting for duty, and I saw that it was with loathing and disgust, as though they were being sent to the slaughter-house. There were cases of resistance, and persecution began. A rising in Bohemia could only be expected by one who had no idea of conditions there. When I decided that I must take some action against Austria, I did not say to myself that I was a patriot and that my country needed me; I simply had a bad conscience at the thought that our people were going to the front and to prison, and that we Members of Parliament, their elected representatives, were sitting at home. I said to myself: "Since you're a Member of Parliament, then go and *do* something!" At the same time I had, of course, to reckon with what might happen to me and my family, but that was all part of the game.

First of all I went twice to Holland. I had a passport for all the countries of Europe; the visa I got for the purpose of accompanying my sister-in-law to the boat; she was going back to America.

I even got a visa the second time. In Holland I collected information, and in particular I got in touch with my English friends, Wickham Steed and Seton Watson. Seton Watson came to Holland to see me; I talked to him for two whole days, and explained the whole of our problem and the value of the breaking up of Austria and transformation of Central Europe. From my information Professor Seton Watson wrote a memorandum for Lord Grey. It was also passed on to the Russians and certain other persons.

Then in December I went to Italy. I had no peace of mind at home, and I wanted to effect a union with my Serb and Croat friends. I gave as a pretext that I wanted to take my daughter Olga to the south; but I did not get the visa. At the Italian frontier the Austrian stationmaster wanted to telegraph to Prague to know if we might go further. Then for the first time in my life I brandished my identity card as a Member of Parliament, and told the man I'd make it hot for him if he tried to prevent my going; he only shrugged his shoulders. Well, there we stood on the platform, and the train in which we had come began to move off into Italy; so we jumped into a carriage and off we went. We had purposely brought very little luggage. Otherwise I might not have managed to get across the frontier. I thought at the time that I should be back in Prague in a few weeks; as a matter of fact I came back exactly four years after the day on which I had crossed the frontier. I had a few thousand crowns with me that Beneš had given me—in fact Beneš financed the beginning of our revolution. I had arranged with Scheiner that the Sokols should let us have a little money from their funds; he also gave me a hope of some money from our fellow countrymen in America, but that was not much as long as the United States were neutral. We did not know which way to turn. With the exception of Scheiner it had not occurred to anyone that we should need money. Before I left Prague I had charged Voska, who was there at the time, to raise something in America for the persecuted Czechs and for the families of those who had been executed. So we were hard up for money all through the war; I don't think there ever was such a cheap revolution in the world before.

In Venice we ran across the journalist Hlaváč, and he gave me the latest news from Vienna. From there I went to Florence and Rome. We stayed near Monte Pincio; I was glad to see Rome again, but I was chiefly occupied in renewing old friendships and seeking new ones. Of course I could not have any definite plan; I had set out from Prague empty-handed, into the void. I saw the Serbs, Croats, and Slovenes, of which there were a number in Rome, but they were not unanimous: there were various points of view—Great Serbian, Great Croatian, Jugoslav. I spent a good deal of time with Supilo and Vošnjak. The Italian agitation for "Dalmazia nostra" was already beginning. Among other people I saw the historian, Professor Lombroso; he clapped his hands when he saw me; there had been stories in the papers of massacres in Prague, and it had been reported that I was shot; he showed me in his files a sheaf of newspaper cuttings and notices about me—dead! I got to know the British Ambassador, and informed him of conditions in Austria; he passed on my letters to Wickham Steed for me. I used to go to these private talks at night, but even so I was watched by Austrian and German spies—the Ambassador called my attention to this, and warned me to take care. Svatkovsky made a journey to see me, and sent my information on to Russia. I went to the Russian Legation; I had to explain to them in detail that it would be a good thing to break up Austria-Hungary —the general belief at the time was that a Danube monarchy was needed as a rampart between Germany and the Balkans. I had' a number of such meetings. I was eager to get home soon; I wanted to hide my note-books and especially a bundle of papers in which there was every possible sort of information about the Habsburg dynasty which I had collected during my term in Parliament. I was afraid that they might find it and imprison my wife on that account; it never crossed my mind that they would take revenge on my daughter Alice. I saw that bundle of notes before me day and night; of course it was eventually confiscated with my books and lost.

I stayed in Rome for about a month; from there I travelled by car with a member of the Italian Diplomatic Service to Genoa and on to Geneva. I was to have meetings in Geneva, chiefly with Professor Ernest Denis, and then to return home. But even the Austrian Consul to whom I went for my visa did not advise me to do that; he talked to me about the war, and was of the opinion that Austria was losing. Soon I got news from two sources: from Beneš in Prague, telling me not to go back because I should be arrested as soon as I set foot on Austrian soil; and from Machar in Vienna telling me that an order had been published that I was to be hanged without further ceremony. So I stayed. It is strange; I was like a machine wound up; I had nothing in my head but our action against Austria. I could see and feel nothing else, just as if I had been hypnotized. I had no mind for anything but the war: how the situation was developing, what changes were taking place on the fronts. After that I would wonder whom to speak to next, and how

235

to approach him, so as to arouse his interest. And then again I would rack my brains as to how I could outwit the frontier officials and get news to and from Prague. It was then that I began to develop insomnia, so much so that I could count on my fingers how many nights out of those four years I really slept.

There were several Czechs in Geneva; Dr. Sychrava was there, then Božinov came, and the engineer Baráček who invented a cypher machine; and there were some students' and workmen's clubs. Later Dürich, the Member of Parliament, arrived. There was connection with Paris, and Képl used to travel to and fro. In Paris Štefánik was beginning his propagands in the salons and clubs; he really had a social mission there, and he succeeded in inspiring people, and winning their interest and their love for us. Twice Benes came from Prague to bring me news. Svatskovsky came too. Then I was in touch with Ernest Denis and with Professor Eisenmann, who was at that time in the French Ministry of War. The Serbian General Consul in Geneva had given me a Serbian passport; I gave my real name, birthplace, and profession, because I did not want to tell needless lies or get myself into difficulties by having a passport under a false name; I was only inscribed as a Serbian citizen. I went to Lyons to have a look at the new French troops in training; I had heard that the French levies were mutinying, and I wanted to see if this was true. I even succeeded in getting into the barracks, where I found the soldiers well disciplined, in good spirits, and in every way reliable. Then I went to see Denis in Paris, and we agreed on the publication of a paper, *La Nation Tchèque*. Štefánik was in hospital having an operation, so I went to see him every day. He was a sentimental fellow, and christened me "Little Father" and would have liked to caress and kiss me; but I did not feel so intimate towards him; the difference in our ages prevented that. I had known him when he was a student in Prague. I remember how once in the winter he came to me all stiff with cold; he had no overcoat so I gave him mine, and then I had to get it altered for him because it was too big. That is fairly typical of the conditions prevailing among us. Remember that nearly all our leading men had a struggle with poverty in their youth, almost with actual hunger and want—but the hungry understand the full, the proverb says.

I lived in the Hotel Richmond in Geneva; I used to go to and fro to Annemasse in France when we had difficulties with the printing of our paper. I even counted on the possibility of having to go to Serbia; that was why I learned to ride a horse, so that in case of need I could ride after the army. And all the time I studied the war and everything connected with it. I had arrived in Geneva without even a sheet of paper, and there I collected another library for myself and my "dove-cot," a set of shelves with divisions and compartments for reviews, newspaper cuttings, and notes; when I moved to London in 1915 I took with me several crates of books and papers, all of them dealing with the war and politics. My relaxations were to go for walks round the lake and to read French novels. I caught up then with French literature, which I had neglected for some years past.

Sending messengers to Prague caused us a great deal of work and worry. I did not want to use the ordinary means which were already familiar to Austrian officialdom, such as sewing a message into a collar or putting it in the heel of a shoe. It was a difficult technical problem for us; for instance, we would hide a slip of paper under the regulator of a watch, bore a suitable hollow into an umbrella, or slip the rolled-up message into a pencil from which a piece of lead had been extracted. It was the engineer Baráček chiefly who performed these feats. A Czech cabinet-maker made us boxes which had not double bottoms but double sides; of course the trick was to make a hollow side which would not sound hollow when it was knocked—our cabinet-maker managed it! Another time we hid our messages in casks of oil, and then we had to mark the casks in an unobtrusive way. Sometimes it didn't come off. Once our messenger was bringing us a message from Prague bound in the inside of the cover of one of Smetana's operas; but during the examination in the train at the frontier he got scared—luckily he found a chance of throwing the volume out of the carriage window.

A still more difficult task was to find messengers and sound them psychologically. They were of all classes, some educated, some quite simple, men and women. I examined each of them separately myself, and told him everything that was likely to happen to him on the way and what difficulties he might find in the way of his mission in Prague; I gave him instructions how to protect himself in whatever case might arise. That was a process of psychological and technical gymnastics, sometimes almost somersaults! Of course the messenger had to buy his ticket to Prague from some other place than Geneva, since Geneva was already suspect. And we had to keep a sharp look-out for Austrian spies. There was one who came to us, but I had been warned against him from Prague; he was a photographer and contributed to our illustrated paper. He had only just arrived when I recognized him and sent him to our people. They welcomed him into their circle, and I think they managed to find out quite a lot about Prague from him. Then there was the curious case of a certain D——. He was an Austrian officer of Moravian origin, and he came to see me at the Hotel Richmond where I was living with an extraordinary story of the Viennese court and the Archduke—if I remember rightly there was even a murder in it. He may have invented it to gain my sympathy, but it was rather characteristic of Vienna. So I published his story as a *feuilleton* in the *Neue Zürcher Zeitung*. I did it to test him, and I saw that he didn't like it at all. I went to Zurich to test what he had told me of his relations with certain English agents there, but I didn't find the people. He wanted at all costs to get to Paris as he had an apparatus for improving the aim in throwing bombs from aeroplanes, which he said he intended to hand over to the Allies. I made it possible for him to live on French territory in Annemasse, where Dr. Sychrava was now living and working, and I sent his plans to Paris; the answer came from Paris that they had hundreds and hundreds of such plans and that they were not interested. Then Mr. D—— disappeared. So I think he, too, must have been a spy, and that, since he could get nothing out of us, he wanted to use us to get into France. When he and I went for walks in the neighbourhood of Annemasse I always carried a loaded revolver with me, and I kept an eye on him, and wouldn't let him get behind me.

Revolution and war are not waged without deceit and lies. It is stupid to try to see in them only heroism—Achilles would not have been possible without Odysseus. That is why a state of society without wars and revolutions would be morally higher. I allowed myself to lie as little as possible, since however careful one may be one gets found out, because one forgets the details one has invented, and so gives oneself away. I had my own method in these matters; when I sent off our messengers I used to take pains to find out everything about their circumstances and abilities so as to give them instructions in the process which would be most useful to them, and prevent their tying themselves up in unnecessary ruses. It is a very curious thing how much people enjoy lying; each knows this about himself, and yet they trust what others tell them! Lying is the companion of violence; therefore lies must be used as little as possible as a means of protection. I am convinced that in practice, even in rebellion, the straight road is the shortest.

And I can tell you this: psychological insight is necessary to politics and to rebellion (and war is the companion of politics). I had the good fortune to know our people at home through and through, hence I knew in advance who would

be the actors in this drama of ours. I had a knowledge of Vienna and of every stratum of society
there from its court down to its beaurocracy and
journalists; that was how I was able to foresee
events, and in the same way I managed, from a
few indications, to grasp the whole position in
Vienna. I had to study the character of our collaborators, and even of our secret adversaries.
Before I went to see anyone important I used to
manage to get hold of the story of his life, so as
to know how to approach him. Of course academic
psychology was no help to me in that, only life
and—novels! For seventy years I have been reading
novels every day; it is only now that I sometimes
omit a day, so as to rest my eyes. I live in fiction. I
should never have held out without it; it contains a
vast amount of experience and knowledge of the
human soul. I think I can read folk pretty well—
it's true that sometimes I misread them. Man is a
damned complicated and puzzling machine. And
each man different!

* * *

When Beneš came to me—and it was high time,
for they would have caught him and imprisoned
him in Prague—I was glad. When he showed me
the passport on which he had crossed the German

frontier—he had slipped out of Austria in secret—
I was almost angry with him for daring to cross a
frontier with such a badly forged passport! It is
absurd, but I was angry and glad at the thought of
those German officials letting him through with
this wretched document! With Beneš with me
things were easier. I had had comparatively little
contact with France, whereas Beneš had studied in
Paris and was more at home there. So Fate had
arranged for us nicely, that we should divide the
work, he in Paris and I elsewhere.

I had got to know Beneš as a colleague at the
University. At the beginning of the war he came
on to the staff of *Time* as a volunteer, saying he
wanted journalistic practice; I saw that he carried
things to practical conclusions. Once he was
coming to my house to see me, but he did not come
there direct; we met in the street when I was
already on my way to the *Time* office. He said his
conscience was pricking him, and that we ought
to do something. I told him I was doing something
already. It was when I had just come back from
my first journey to Holland. Then we went to the
office together, and on the way I told him all that
I had done so far and all that I had in my mind. I
remember as if it were to-day how, as we came
down from Letná Gardens at the point where almost
the whole of Prague lies spread out before one, the

prophecy of Libuse[1] came into my mind. . . . Of course our first concern was money, and Beneš promised immediately that he would raise some. And he brought it.

In Switzerland I got to know him better—and I can tell you that without Benes we should not have had our Republic. There was complete agreement between us on the main issues; even when I was not there Benes decided everything, exactly as we should have decided after talking over the whole matter together. Once, later, he came from Paris to see me in London and gave an account of what he was doing and how our work was developing, how our aims were slowly being realized. And when he had finished I said to him: "Benes, you and I are going to be friends."

*　*　*

In 1915, on the five hundredth anniversary of the burning of John Huss, I appeared with Denis at the Reformation Hall in Geneva, with Lucien Gautier as Chairman, at a public demonstration against Austria. We chose that day so as to prove in the eyes of the world the historical continuity of

[1] Libuse, first Queen of the Czechs, standing on one of the hills overlooking the site of Prague, declared: "I see a city whose glory shall reach the stars."—TRANSLATOR'S NOTE.

our country's history. I knew already that either we must win or I should never go back to Austria.

During my stay in Geneva my son Herbert died. He caught typhus from the Galician refugees. Then Alice was imprisoned—that was to do with the affair of the button. There was a Czech living in Geneva who was a Social Democrat and was worrying because his Party in Bohemia was not being active enough against Austria. So on his own account he sent a messenger, a lady, and gave her a secret message concealed in a red button which she was simply to give to Dr. Soukup. The lady travelled happily to Prague and sent her father-in-law, a workman, to deliver the button. Of course our people were suspicious of him; they thought he was an *agent provocateur* sent by the police, and the long and short of it was that the button got into the hands of the police, who proceeded to prosecute the people named in the message it held. A petition against Alice's imprisonment was presented to the Austrian Government by the women of America. I learned by hearsay that my wife was ill; I was afraid that Alice would not be able to survive imprisonment; then the American papers published the news that my youngest son, John, who was in the army, had been, or was going to be, hanged because of me. All this, and other things too, got on my nerves, but it did not break me down. I really lived as if in a dream. I saw nothing but the aim we had before us. When my friends tried to comfort me I put on a heroic air as if it were nothing . . . it was all part of the day's work, I used to say.

A man can stand a good deal, everything, in fact, if he has an aim before him and has once resolved that he will pursue it sincerely, come what may. Sincerity is the secret of the world and of life; it is a religious and moral holiness.

London

I went from Geneva to London for the first time in April 1915 to meet Wickham Steed and Seton Watson, Professor Sarolea, and some other people, and there I wrote a memorandum for the British Government and the other Allies. I had been warned that a spy was going to travel with me in the sleeping car from Geneva to Paris, and that I had better take care. Very well, I thought, so long as I know who I'm travelling with! So I did not change either the date of my journey or the number of my carriage; I simply put my portfolio under my pillow and steamed out of the station.

I moved my headquarters to London at the end of September of the same year. Beneš and Štefánik were already working in Paris. So we arranged it like that. The political centre of the Allies was really Paris; England had more weight in economic matters.

It is natural that I should know the Anglo-Saxons better than any other nation; that came as a matter of course through my marriage with an American. But I had learnt French before I knew English; I had read a lot and knew French literature so well that I never went to Paris before the war at all; money was not abundant, and I preferred to visit the countries whose culture was less known to me. Only on my way to and from America I used to stay in a French port and explore its surroundings.

I liked being in London. In a great city like that you can be alone even when you are among millions of people. In 1915 I stayed at first in a boarding-house at Hampstead, Miss Brown's, 4 Holford Road. I used to ride into town on the top of a bus and watch the swarms of people and traffic. I didn't like using a car; I said to myself, why pay more when you get there just the same for a little? Our people said I ought to have my own car, "because of my position." In town I used to have my meals at a Lyons; it was cheap, you could get a good dinner for ten to fifteen pence When I had guests and had to think of my position, I used to take them to the Café Royal. At the boarding-house I suffered a lot from the cold; you know those English open fires don't give very much heat. In the autumn of 1916 Olga found a little furnished house belonging to a certain Pastor Wilder, who had been recalled to America; it was in Hampstead, too, 21 Platt's Lane. It had every convenience you can think of, including a cook, so after that I used to have my meals at home. I used to walk about Hampstead Heath, sometimes even at night when I was worried, when, for instance, there was talk of a separate peace with Austria. Once I cut my head open, too, when I collided with a lamp-post in a London fog. Periodically the sirens would go off—it was the alarm against the German air-raids; at that signal everyone had to take cover in cellars or tunnels. . . . I much preferred to stay in the garden and watch it; once we saw two burning Zeppelins over Hendon; another time thirty-six flying machines flew over amid a rain of bursting shells. It was a glorious spectacle. I often found pieces of shell in the garden. While I was in Brighton a German submarine bombarded the town.

Once burglars tried to break into our house; the police thought that they were after my papers, and advised me to have alarm-bells fixed to all the doors, windows, and fireplaces. While I was in Switzerland I had had a curious eruption on my shoulders, and the doctor there thought that it was from poison. In England I got it again on my neck; they had to cut it open, and then they sent me to Bournemouth to recover by the sea. The English doctors also said it was due to poisoning, caused by my linen and manipulated by my political adversaries. I thought it was simply lack of fresh air; so later when I was in America I started riding again; it is said that in riding a horse you breathe in twice as much fresh air as walking. I had influenza several times. . . . One manages to survive a great deal. I was aware that some spy or fanatic might try to murder me, and when Beneš came to see me I prepared him for it. I wasn't alarmed at all, and I simply arranged with him that if I died he should use the fact to further our propaganda. I drew up a kind of will, too—a sad affair, because I had nothing to leave except some of my writings—and debts!

On my arrival in London I had difficulties with my passport. I had obtained a Serbian passport in Geneva, as you will remember; but, so as to avoid contradicting myself under repeated cross-questionings, I had filled in everything except my nationality quite truthfully, born at Hodonín in Moravia, professor, and so on. No one paid any attention to it till I went for money to the London branch of the Swiss bank where I had deposited my money in Geneva. There the cashier shook his head over my passport; he was a German Swiss and was strong in geography, and he pointed out that Moravia is not in Serbia, and more to the same effect. However, I was able to get the better of him. I said to him: "Since you know so much geography, you ought to know that the Morava is a river in Serbia—and moreover, what does my passport matter to you?" All the same, I changed my account to another bank. At Hampstead a detective used to follow me for a long time; he had somehow got wind of that passport of mine. By this time I had been appointed professor at King's College, London University (I had not much taste for the post, but it was a good thing for me to hold it), and Asquith, then Prime Minister, was to give the inaugural lecture of my course; however, he was ill and sent Lord Robert Cecil instead. Of course it was all in the newspapers, so I showed it to the detective and said: "If your Prime Minister trusts me, I should think you can trust me too." But it didn't have any effect on him—and of course he was in the right. I asked Seton Watson to arrange it for me somehow at Scotland Yard, and after that they left me in peace. The man at the head of Scotland Yard, Sir Basil Thompson, got interested in me.

After that my relations with the police were only friendly. But all through the war I had the feeling that the Austrian police were hunting me; even at home, as President, I have sometimes had the feeling—it is only recently that I have been free of dreams like that.

*   *   *

To-day I am astonished that I had the strength to work as I did then. Every week I used to write, or rather dictate, an article for the *Sunday Times*, using my many sources of information and my own ability to draw conclusions. I wrote for other papers, too, *The Nation*, *Spectator*, *New Europe*; I sent notes through our Press bureau; I prepared I don't know how many memoranda; and the letters that I had to write! Then there was my course at the University, lectures at various clubs, at Cambridge, and at Oxford, where I stayed with the Cretan expert, Sir Arthur Evans, and got to know Miljukov and Vinogradov. I went to Edinburgh to have a talk with the Belgian Consul, Professor Sarolea, and his secretary, Mrs. West; they published a nice paper called *Everyman*, which took an interest in our cause. I used to go to the Foreign Office to see Sir George Clerk, who later became British Minister in Prague, and the former Ambassador to Vienna, Sir Maurice Bunsen; and of course I went to see journalists and professors. There were Saturdays at Wickham Steed's, where newspaper men, officers, and diplomats used to meet. Everyone who came to London used to call on Steed and Madame Rose— she wrote good articles in the *Morning Post*. I can't even remember how many people I visited and tried to interest. I did not thrust myself on people in official positions so long as we were not able to win over public opinion. At first I was empty-handed and could promise nothing. I only had my argument that the dismemberment of Austria-Hungary was to the interest of the whole of Europe. I tried to contrive that every day the newspapers should publish something against Austria, and about us; we had to make our cause known; it was not enough to be in political contact with a few people in high office. And that was all very hard work, overwhelmingly hard. Then there were journeys, visits, meetings, and lectures, articles and letters, and always our post to be sent off and worried over when the English police made difficulties about it. That happened more often after the button affair, when we received couriers from America; for as long as America was neutral American citizens could still go to Vienna and even to Prague.

I had my own principles in the matter of propaganda, and I think they were right: not to abuse the Germans, not to underrate the enemy, not to

distort facts or make boasts; not to make empty
promises, and not to approach people as a beggar;
to let facts speak for themselves, and use them as
evidence: so-and-so is in your interest, and therefore
your duty; to influence by ideas and arguments and
remain personally in the background; not to be an
opportunist, not to snatch at the things which
pass with the day, to have one plan and one standard
in everything; and one thing more—not to be
importunate. Equally important was not to accept
money from anyone but our own people, even when
we were badly in need. Sometimes our cash-box
would be nearly empty and Beneš would telegraph
that we need so much—and often on the very
same day a cheque would come from our people
in America. Sometimes at the beginning I would
be sorry that there were so few of our people in
the outside world, but that proved a good thing—
there were no quarrels to speak of.

To lie and exaggerate is the worst propaganda of
all. I will give you an example: when our friend
Seton Watson was young, and was preparing an
historical study of the Calvinists in Hungary, he
had no idea—hardly anyone in Western Europe
had—of the nationalistic policy of the Magyars;
he liked the Magyars. While he was collecting his
material in Pesth, he came across some documents
on the Slovaks and asked about them, as he thought

253

he would like to go and see them. "There are no Slovaks," the Magyars told him. "Those are just a few shepherds in the mountains." But Seton Watson got to know some Slovaks; he got more information from them, and went to Slovakia[1] to see for himself. When he got back to Vienna he said to Wickham Steed, in round-eyed astonishment: "Think of it, the Magyars lied to me about it, lied to me!" And that was what induced him to begin his study of the national problems of the Slovaks and Jugoslavs, and to become the authority on Magyarization and Magyar policy. A lie never pays either in politics or in private life.

* * *

Once or twice I have had extraordinary strokes of luck. The first time was in 1916, when Štefánik arranged an interview for me with Briand. I had actually bought my ticket on the Channel steamer *Sussex* to go to Paris, when Beneš wired me not to come as the appointment was postponed; so I cancelled my passage. And on that journey the *Sussex* was torpedoed by the Germans and sunk.

The second time was when I was on my way to Russia, and wanted to sail from the English port of Amble to Bergen in Norway. I waited for the boat at Amble but she didn't come; she had been

[1] Then Upper Hungary.—TRANSLATOR'S NOTE.

sunk; if I had gone by her I should also have missed Štefánik, who was just coming back from Russia and had news for me. So I went back to London, where Štefánik was waiting for me; Beneš came from Paris too. A few days later I took the boat from Aberdeen. We were escorted by two torpedo-boats. During the night the boat suddenly heeled over and swung round so quickly that everything was flung this way and that. In the morning the captain told me that we had only just avoided a floating mine—the boat swung round just at the last minute.

I had to get a new passport to go to Russia, under a false name, naturally. I had chosen myself a Danish name, Madwig; I took a Danish name because my wife, whose name was Garrigue, came to America from Denmark, and Madwig occurred to me; it was the name of a Danish philologist. I thought out the whole story of my life and learnt it off by heart so that I should not be caught out contradicting myself if I fell into the hands of the Germans: I was of Danish origin, but had lived in the United States since my early childhood, and so on. But Sir Basil Thompson advised me to change the name; I don't know why. He himself suggested Thomas George Marsden, and I travel about the world under that name even to-day. Sir Basil also advised me to be extremely careful when

I went to Sweden, as German spies were active there, and if I were denounced to the Swedish authorities they might hand me over to Austria or at least intern me as an act of neutrality to Austria. So when I got to Stockholm I didn't even go to an hotel but walked about the streets all day with Bohdan Pavlů, who had come from Petrograd to meet me.

I prepared for that journey very carefully; I removed every trace of my identity. I ripped from my clothes every mark of a Prague or London firm; and three times I went through every piece of paper and every scrap of clothing that I was taking with me, and examined them minutely to be sure that there was nothing to betray me. But when I was in Russia I found among my linen a collar on which the London laundry had written in indelible ink my full name: MASARYK! And I had so relied on my caution and my practical sense!

I have often thought over such fateful moments as this in my life. I have never understood the idea of an aristocratic Providence, as though I had some special right to its protection. Many people have luck as great as mine, perhaps everyone has it. It is another thing to see the workings of Providence in the development of a State or nation. Of course, States and nations are made up of individuals, individuals are the expression and the instruments of the whole. That is a difficult problem; I do not claim to be able to explain it clearly. It is a hard puzzle for a philosopher.

1917

I had gone to Russia partly at the request of the Russian Branch of our National Council; the work of unifying our action in the Allied countries was urgent. There was the recruiting and organization of our volunteers from the Russian prison camps to see to, and especially their formation into an independent "Corpus," which was in reality our national army fighting against Austria. Our greatest obstacle in this respect came from the Russian bureaucrats—bureaucracy, you know, exists not only in offices but in armies. We had to wait until after the fall of the Tsar for things to get easier for us, and were chiefly helped by the new Minister for Foreign Affairs, Miljukov, whom I knew well. So I chose this moment for going to Russia. But almost as soon as I got there Miljukov resigned and soon civil war broke out. And in the midst of this complete upheaval we had to organize our political and military action. It was bad luck.

When I arrived in Russia there was shooting everywhere. In Petrograd my rooms were in the Morskaya, opposite the Telegraph and Telephone

257

Office, over which there was a stiff fight. The office of our Branch National Council was on the Znamen-skaya, so I used to go there on foot from my rooms near the Winter Palace. Our people were afraid I should get hurt, and assigned me as "bodyguard" the Czech prisoner Hůza, who was cook to one of the members of the Branch. They led him to me in his apron, and said that he was to accompany me everywhere. It was a long time before I could get used to him. I had been in the habit of doing everything for myself—I even cleaned my own boots—and now here was a fellow who insisted on doing everything for me. I had to get accustomed to it.

But even with a bodyguard it was far from safe in Petrograd; and how could he really have helped me if a bullet had hit us? Our people insisted on my going to Moscow; it was quiet there, and the Branch was to follow me. So I set off, accompanied by Kódl, whose name is known from the novels about our legion. But as soon as I got to Moscow the fighting broke out there. We could hear it even from the railway station. I left Hůza at the station to bring my boxes after me in a cab and set out on foot to the Hotel National in the main square, where I had booked a room. I reached the square and ran into a cordon of soldiers. "Where are you going?" the officer called to me. "To the Hotel National," I said. "Out of the question," he said, "they're shooting there." I looked at the square and saw that they were shooting from both sides. On one side the Bolshevists had occupied the theatre; Kerensky's soldiers were holding the other side, and both parties were shooting with rifles and machine-guns. The officer advised me to go to the Metropole. I went. A man was hurrying along in front of me and slipped in through the great doors which were opened for him. It was the Hotel Metropole. I tried to slip in after him, but they slammed the doors in my face. So I knocked at them and called: "What are you doing? Open the door!" "Are you staying here?" the porter called back, "we can't let you in otherwise. We're all booked up." I didn't want to tell a lie, so I shouted at him: "Don't be a fool, and let me in!" He stopped talking and let me in.

The Hotel Metropole was a huge hotel de luxe for foreigners and rich people who came to Moscow to go on the razzle. At that moment it held, including the staff, about five hundred people. In the attic of the hotel were about fifty of Kerensky's cadets, who were shooting down on the Bolshevists, and the Bolshevists in the theatre were shooting back at them. When I got inside the hotel the manager, or whoever he was, came up to me and said "You must leave here. We've no room for you, and we can't give you anything to eat." "I'm not going to leave," I said, "and I don't want you to give me anything. Don't you bother about me." So they let me sit down in my fur coat, just as I was, and took no more notice of me. All the time the Bolshevists were firing on the hotel; the guests rushed into the cellar, where they were given their midday and evening meals. I didn't go. In the evening the hotel cook came up to me; he looked at me and thought to himself how queer I was; then he began to talk to me, and told me he was expecting his father-in-law on a visit from the country and had got a room ready for him; but since his father-in-law couldn't get to the hotel while things were like this I could have the room. And after that he even gave me supper.

The room was on the second or third floor, round a corner where bullets could only penetrate if they ricochetted from the houses opposite. I dragged the mattress from the bed and put it on the floor in a corner, and there I slept. In the daytime I wandered about the hotel, and wondered what Hûza was doing, and the Moscow Czechs who were expecting me. Out of the hotel I could not go; the telephone was in the vestibule, where the shooting was worst, so that we had no communication with the outside. You know it was strange; I have seldom lived through days which seemed so long. The first day it was not so bad; they were only shooting with rifles and machine-guns; but after a day or two the Bolshevists began to fire on the hotel with cannon placed outside the town. Soon the front of the hotel and all the upper floors were shot away. The guests changed their quarters to the cellars. I really could not stay there with them; there was such an awful smell and noise, children and women were crying. One of the guests was a Pole who had been through the bombardment of Przemysl; he said that this was even worse. But in spite of that I crawled—I had literally to crawl because of the heaps of debris and the continual shooting—back to my little room for the night.

One picture I shall always remember. I can see it as if it were yesterday. I stood in the corner of my room by the window, and peered out into the street to see how it looked. And I saw a youth run out into the street and try to cross it. He raced along and suddenly he fell down with his face to the ground, his arms flung out wide. I thought to myself, "If I were a doctor I should know by the way he fell where he's been hit." There he lay on the pavement with his face to the stones and his sheepskin cap rolled away from him a little farther down the street. From under his face flowed a little stream of blood, then a second, and a third—I counted them, there were seven. While I was

261

watching a raven flew down, perched on the cap, and looked at the boy. I felt so terrified lest it should begin to tear him with its beak, but I couldn't do anything to drive it away. . . . I saw that there was a Red Cross ambulance round the corner, but no one came for the boy because there was shooting all the time. Still, in spite of that, they took pity on him; they came for him, waving their Red Cross, and carried him away. I don't know if he was still alive. I remember so many pictures like that. . . .

Since the hotel telephone was placed in the entrance hall where bullets were flying, we were forbidden to use it; but later, in spite of this, I crept to the telephone box and rang up our people to tell them where I was; they had all thought I must be dead. Then Hůza tried one evening to bring me some clean clothes, but he had to turn back. One night, during the bombardment, Kerensky's cadets withdrew from the hotel, but the Bolshevists went on firing. The hotel surrendered, and the Bolshevists agreed that next day (a Saturday, I think) the guests could leave. The Russian guests chose a Pole to represent them at the parley with the Bolshevists, the foreign guests—there were about forty of them—chose me. We had all the weapons there were were in the hotel brought and piled together; but the Pole hid some of the loaded revolvers and the ammunition in case a massacre should break out—in which case it would be of little importance whether we defended ourselves or not. He was chiefly afraid there might be a rush to take possession of the women, and that would have led to a general butchery. Some of us knew of the hiding-place of the weapons. The Bolshevists came, occupied the hotel, and collected the arms. They were a motley garrison, with their rifles slung on with rope and other queer rig. They put us under guard. One of the soldiers snatched at the ring which fastened my tie. It was a white metal ring with a red stone set in it; our boys had made it out of fuses and given it to me as a "souvenir," but because I don't wear rings except my wedding ring, I used it to fasten my tie. I showed it to the soldier so that he could see it was only lead and glass and told him it was a souvenir. "I want it," he said. "Give it to me." I wouldn't. And I asked him jokingly if he would let me out soon. "I'll let you out if I like," he said, "and if I like I'll cut your throat." However, he didn't cut my throat. Some of the guests bribed the guard, but I'm not a good hand at bribing, it's so humiliating.

The worst thing of all was when the guards got drunk on the wine they found in the cellar. I went to their commander and asked him to change them. He was willing to hear reason, and sent another guard. After a long night a commission came to

263

examine our passports; the leader of it was a student, to judge by his clothes. Among the guests at the hotel was the Socialist Lotyš, who knew my book on Marxism. He helped me a lot to avoid difficulties.

So after about a week I got out. I went to stay with fellow countrymen of mine, and began to work again at the organization of our "Corpus." Our boys went to look at the bombarded hotel where I had been staying; one of them took a key from the hotel, and when he got home he put it in the museum at Turčanský Svatý Martín.

Presently I left Moscow for Kiev, as our "Corpus" was encamped in the suburbs. I put up at the Hotel Paris on the Kreshchatik. But scarcely had I arrived when the Bolshevists surrounded Kiev, and when the time allowed for surrender was past they opened artillery fire on the city. Dr. Girsa, who was the doctor at the hospital, took me to the Georgijevskij Hospital, saying that I should be safer there; but the meetings of our Branch Council were at the Hotel Paris, so that it was six of one and half a dozen of the other, for I had to go there on foot every day. Once a shell fell in the room next to the one where we were conferring. It hit the wall, fell to the floor, and then lay still; it didn't explode! It was as long as my forearm. No one was wounded; only a piece of plaster hit on the head a member of the family who were dining there!

Then the Bolshevists advanced into the city and fighting began in the streets. The way to the office of our Branch led across the main boulevard, along a cross street called, I think, Prorjeznaja. One day I was walking with Hůza along this street across which there was shooting. We took cover against the houses on the side from which the bullets were flying—it is true that tiles and chimney-pots might drop on us; but it was the lesser evil. A shell dropped and exploded in the court of a house close by; we went to look at it.

When we reached the main boulevard an officer came striding towards us waving his hand. "No thoroughfare!" he shouted. "Danger! Back!" Along the boulevard there was a regular hail of bullets on the pavement. I looked at Hůza: "If we go back," I said, "we're just as likely to get hit, so let's go on!" and we raced across the boulevard.

One day Klecanda and I went to the railway station to meet the commander of the Bolshevists. When we were in front of the station there was a whizz, and an inch in front of our faces a bullet hit a telegraph pole. Close to us in the entrance two boys were playing with a loaded rifle; it went off, shot one of them, and the bullet flew on close to us.

The only time I was really afraid was when the soldiers in Moscow got drunk; terrible things might have happened then. Otherwise I was not afraid,

265

or if I was I gave no sign of it; for the sake of our soldiers that was a thing I must not do. How could I have authority over them if they saw that I was afraid? There is really a lot that could be told about this time, and my individual experiences then, but I have forgotten many of the details, and to be quite frank, I don't care to remember them. My head is full of quite other details now. . . .

With the Soldiers in Russia

In Russia, believe me, I had to work even harder than in England; there was no more writing now; it was talk and negotiations, or rather talk, for without a lot of palaver there's no getting anything done in Russia. Those Russian conversations lasting from morning till night! I used not to get out into the air till God knows what time. And then that endless travelling about—to the Russian Staff Headquarters, to our different regiments—it was a very fatiguing business. Once when I was in the train on the way from Kiev, the carriage in which I was sitting had an accident; the axle broke, or something of that sort; fortunately the train was just slowing down to enter a station, so nothing happened except that we had to travel the rest of the way standing crowded together in the next carriage.

THE WAR AND AFTER

Our difficulties in Russia were many; the greatest was with the Russian bureaucracy, which could not understand our cause; they treated us as traitors to our Emperor, and whoever had betrayed his Emperor might also betray the Tsar. We wanted them to allow us to form our prisoners of war into a volunteer army against the Germans; and when we had been allowed to form several regiments we tried to get permission to weld these into a "Corps" which would be under our sole authority. And you know, I'm really not surprised that they didn't like the idea. They were afraid that if they granted us permission they would also have to grant it to the Poles, and they distrusted them. And besides, they had not enough arms and equipment for their own troops, and would have had to equip ours, too. And many Russians did not want our men to be soldiers at all; they needed our prisoners as well-trained workmen in the factories and mines, on the railways and fields. So I was obliged to go with Klecanda and others of our friends to General Headquarters and to all sorts of Ministers—that was a bitter pill to swallow.

Miljukov, who would have been the most likely to fall in with our wishes, had just resigned, as I said. I negotiated with the generals, with Brusilov, Alexjejev, and in particular with Duchonin (he was head of the Russian General Staff and a good soldier), and it was with him that we finally fixed things up. Perhaps our greatest help came from public opinion when our men fought so well at the battle of Zborov. Just then I was negotiating about our Corps at the Russian General Staff in Mogilev; I talked to a number of people, especially Brusilov —he bowed deeply and said: "I bow before your soldiers." After that I was glad to be able to do something for him when he was an exile taking the cure at Carlsbad. After his death his wife sent me his personal *eikon*, wrapped round in cloth which had been torn by bullets—he had carried it about with him everywhere for protection, and he had shown it to me.

When at last we had got our Corps, Duchonin asked me whom we wanted to command it, and I named General Šokorov, a reliable military official. Soon after this the Bolshevists killed Duchonin and dishonoured his corpse. I went to his funeral, and there his wife told me that he had wanted to command our army himself. How could it have entered my head that the Chief of the General Staff would think it worth while to command our Corps! But at least we can show our gratitude to his widow for his goodwill and the good opinion he had of our soldiers.

As soon as we had our Corps, difficulties began with the Bolshevists. We had agreed on armed

268

neutrality, and I had got them to consent to send us across Siberia to France. When I went to Siberia they wanted either to disarm us or win us over to their side. All this meant negotiations and again negotiations with the Commissars, with the soldiers, with all manner of folk.

Other difficulties lay in the nature of our own people. We had above all in Russia our old half-Russianized emigrants. Every group of emigrants takes on something of the psychology of the country in which it is settled. The psychology of our colony in Paris, in America, in Russia, was in each case quite different—and one had to take that into account. A few influential countrymen of ours in Russia had adopted the whole programme of the old Tsarist system. When I arrived some of them informed against me at the different ministries, and here and there they had influence over our people. So all that had to be put in order.

Then there were some difficulties among our own soldiers. We had volunteers from the Czech colony in Russia, and volunteers from among the prisoners of war; firstly there were disagreements between members of the original Czech "Družina," the volunteers from Serbia and the Dobrudja, and the new regiments recruited from among the Czech prisoners in the Russian prisoners' camps, and these had to be settled. Then there were disputes over the direction which our march should take: over the Caucasus to the Rumanian front, or via Archangel to France. Thirdly there was disagreement as to whether the words of command should be given in Russian or Czech; fourthly as to whether the officers should mess with the men or not. It was things like these that I had to attend to. What did I say to them? I told them it didn't matter a tinker's curse what was the language of command provided orders were obeyed; that it didn't matter whether the officers and men ate together—they could mess where they liked, but let them see that the commissariat was well managed. There were some demagogic officers who used to mess with the men and make speeches to them over the table, and there were some soldiers who didn't want to go to war. There were difficulties in provisioning the army, and all round us the Russian army was disintegrating and falling to pieces. That was the state of things in which I organized my "Corpus."

You must realize that our prisoners of war had become demoralized to a certain extent. That was altogether natural: there is an element of humiliation and injustice in captivity which cripples a man in a way—he hasn't his roots in his native soil. When once your soldier has thrown away his gun he wants to have done with war. The recruiting of volunteers from the prison camps sometimes did not go very smoothly. There were commanders of camps, chiefly non-Russian, who put every conceivable obstacle in the way of our recruiting. The manifestos circulated in the camps calling on our prisoners to volunteer for the field were full of ideals which tended rather to frighten them off: "You will suffer hunger, you will get full of lice in the trenches"—that was the sort of reward that they were promised if they joined our army. While all the time, of course, they wanted to have enough to eat and to live a more human life than that of prisoners of war. And then there were those who quarrelled with their officers because they held that a volunteer must not obey blindly; the demagogues fostered that opinion; they made soldiers' councils and conventicles on the Bolshevist model, and wanted to run the army by vote. All this was natural but it sometimes made things difficult. We had one colonel of this sort, a Russian, who had his mouth full of Huss and his brethren, because he thought he would get promotion that way. I passed him over, and his regiment nearly mutinied. There was a great deal of this kind of thing. Those of our men who became Bolshevized carried on agitation against the army and against the loan that was being floated to finance it; but when the Germans were approaching Kiev these men hastily joined

271

our army—the army had already become a protection for us.

I can tell you this: your Czech is a good soldier when he is under fire; then he is brave and clever so that few are his equal. He can get out of every kind of tight corner; but when he's out of it, he manages to get into one by himself. He cannot hold out indefinitely, and he is not a success when he has nothing to do. We had an example of this before the Siberian march, and again at the end of the Siberian campaign. But even a better equipped and organized army than ours would have fought that campaign no better than we. My one concern was that they should still be good soldiers when they got to France; and all this business of brotherhood and the rights of a volunteer army did not matter so long as they remained an effective fighting force. We hastily started courses for superior officers, drill for the men, and all manner of different workshops and activities for them—tailoring, shoemaking, pork-butchery, printing, sports and theatre, post and bank—so as to keep them occupied and prevent their running away. They had to see after the commissariat and that was very difficult; the peasants in the Ukraine did not like to sell for paper roubles; they said they had sold to the Germans for nails; paper money had no value for them; they had returned to the primitive method of

272

trade by barter. This part of our business went better in Siberia. Of course as soon as our boys were under fire they were such soldiers as you seldom see—they were fighting for their lives.

Our soldiers were fond of me, and acknowledged me as their commander-in-chief, mainly, I think, because I was severe with them—in the army one has to be frank—and perhaps because I was not afraid. The boys went in crowds to look at the Hotel Metropole, all damaged by the shooting, as it had been when I stayed there, and told each other whole legends about me; they said I wasn't afraid of anything. Well, you know, I was frightened now and then, but I didn't let anyone know; it was entirely for the sake of the boys that I used to walk about the streets while the firing was going on. But they did not recognize the professor in me. I was so happy with them; I noticed a great deal in common between soldiers and children. Soldiers, like children, must be treated with fairness, frankness, openness; because they must obey even if it means their death, the man whom they obey must really win their respect and without hypocrisy. Military parades are, in fact, much more for the soldiers than for their officers. I like soldiers, even though I don't like war.

My greatest problem was to decide where our Corps could be used with the greatest effect. The

Russian fronts had ceased to be; but there were stationed in the west five hundred thousand well-equipped German soldiers, because the Germans didn't trust the Bolshevists. At the beginning the Bolshevists would have gone with us against the Germans, but the Allies did not want that, and rightly; then Lenin made peace with the Germans against the will of Trotsky. And I ask you, how could anyone imagine that after that we could fight our way home through the German front—with fifty thousand soldiers, almost no artillery, inadequate equipment, an entirely deficient commissariat, in the heart of a country in full revolution—or wage a war of extermination against the Bolshevists? Tsarism had fallen, the whole administration had disintegrated, the vast land of Russia was overwhelmed by revolution—with fifty thousand soldiers we could not hope to suppress a great movement called into being by the defects of the old régime! France, in the autumn of 1917, wanted to throw our soldiers on to the Rumanian front. So I went to have a look at the front at Jassy; I found scarcely any fighting going on; they just fired a shot or two in my honour, and the Germans replied in an equally unwarlike way. I had talks with the Rumanian and French officers, and heard that their men were getting no meat at all and not even enough bread; their commissariat was giving

274

out. I sensed the fact that Rumania was thinking of peace—and I was right. And what would have happened to us then? So I decided not to go there, even though I had a disagreement with Clemenceau about it.

So the only possible and reasonable course was to transfer our soldiers to the French front, where every man was needed. And I saw that could not be done via Archangel; the transport from there was bad and the Germans would have torpedoed our troop ships at sea in a twinkling. The shortest way to France and home was the longest: across Siberia and round the world. So I arranged that and travelled ahead myself across Siberia like a good quartermaster, to let our boys see that the thing could be done. I arranged with the Bolshevists— with their first Generalissimo and then with the Commissar Fritch, who was a University professor—that it should be an armed neutrality. Our soldiers were to travel with their arms: I had that in black and white. I issued the following instructions: they were not to mix themselves up in Russian internal affairs if we ever wanted to get out of Russia; but if any Slav party rose against them they were to defend themselves. With Germans and Hungarians we were already in a state of war, since I had got the French to declare our army officially a part of theirs; the only people who

275

could get in the way of our soldiers were the Bolshevists—that was why I said "Slav party." Neutrality went without saying, since the Bolshevists were providing us with food, or at least were putting no obstacles in the way of our foraging.

I left Moscow on March 7th, my birthday. By the kindness of Lady Paget I got a place in the English Red Cross train which was carrying the English Red Cross Mission out of Russia; I was only given a hard bench in the train—so of course Hůza managed to get me a mattress in Moscow. The journey lasted a month. On the way I thought out and wrote down my book *The New Europe*; I studied my English travelling companions; I had debates with the guard on the train, who was a Bolshevist. Once the train had to stop because there was fighting in the country ahead of us. Sometimes our fuel ran out and wood had to be cut for the locomotive—Hůza could beat them all at that.

I was in a hurry to get to America for another reason. I was expecting a Peace Conference; but I had to stop a little in Japan to get into touch with the European Allies and inspect the Japanese army; our soldiers, or at least a part of them, were coming to Japan to be shipped for Europe. I was not able to study Japan. I had no time to look round me.

276

THE WAR AND AFTER

It was a heavy piece of work in Russia, but fine work. It meant that we should not go home empty-handed; now we had something real, something of our very own, our army, the first actual though extra-territorial part of our future State.

The End of the War

I sailed from Japan to Vancouver on the *Empress of Asia*. In America our countrymen were waiting for me everywhere, and American newspaper-men as well—I had to get accustomed to the enthusiasm of my American reception. The whole country lived in a state of fiery excitement during the war; it was new to them; they felt a new bond with Europe and with the whole world. Their enthusiastic welcome to me was partly caused by the popularity of our legions who had by now begun to fight their way by force of arms across Russia and Siberia. I knew our soldiers; I knew that they would come through it successfully; but the Americans had an astonishing admiration for every kind of heroism, so the march of our fifty thousand across a whole continent made a great impression.

It was my fourth visit to America. The first was when I followed Miss Garrigue in 1878; and I had been twice to lecture, in 1902 and 1907. So I have seen America grow from her pioneer days.

Yes, I like America. Not that I like the countryside —our own is prettier. The American countryside is—how shall I put it?——it's like American fruit; it always seems to me that their fruit is somehow more bitter than ours, and that ours is sweeter and mellower to the taste. To the American farmer, equipped with machines, the soil is a factory, not an object of love as it is to our people.

What I like about America is the frankness of the people. Of course there are good and bad folk there, just as there are with us; but they are more frank about it. Your American racketeer is completely ruthless; he is frankly a plunderer without any ceremony; he does not screen himself behind moral or patriotic pretexts. The good ones are equally energetic on behalf of all they consider good, whether it be a humanitarian, religious, or cultural issue. They are more enterprisingly good than we. There is a pioneering element about it which is in keeping with their untamed soil.

The speed and scale of their industry does not surprise me. Since they have to supply goods to a hundred million of their people they have had to accustom themselves to producing on a large scale; it is the result of their vast dimensions. As for their capitalism, I don't see that it differs from ours; they have their millionaires in dollars as we have them in crowns; it is only that the scale is larger. People talk of the race for dollars, as if we were any better than they in that. Of course the difference is that in Europe the race is more for farthings than for dollars, and that we run it in a shamefaced way, as though we were cadging for a tip. In this respect Europe is less reckless but dirtier.

As for America being machine-ridden, machines have a good side as well as a bad, so have rationalization and things of that sort. If machines can take the place of man in rough and exhausting work, that is all to the good. One should think more of that and less of financial gain. The speed of American work was strange to me; I myself need what you might call a free margin, in any work I do, so that I can think the thing out in an orderly way. A Czech workman may be less quick, but he works well and accurately; quality ranks with us before quantity. The Americans have more respect for physical labour than we. Your American student goes harvesting in his vacation or works as a waiter; with us intellectual and especially academic culture is almost overrated. But in comparison with our people, the American workman is freer and has more elbow-room; if he is smart he will have his own Ford car and bungalow; on the other hand, there is no Socialism in our sense of the word.

The fact that so-called Americanism is invading

Europe does not matter. We have been "Europeanizing" America for several centuries, and they have the right to do the same. We become Americanized, but don't forget that America is getting more and more Europeanized. I have read that two million Americans come to Europe every year; if Europe has anything of value for their life, they take it back with them. When you read the most recent American authors you see how severely they judge the mistakes and platitudes of American life—I only wish our Czech authors were as frank about our mistakes! In future America and Europe must balance and compensate each other. In short, America furnished me with ample food for observation and study; I learnt there much, very much, of value.

* * *

During my stay in America I was consciously preparing myself for the Peace Conference. In particular we had to strengthen the union of Czechs and Slovaks. A second task was to reach an agreement with the Ruthenians, so that they should declare themselves a part of our State. That was a brand-new project which first came up in America; I saw at once what it would mean for us if we had a territorial bridge to the coming democratic Russia or to the Ukraine. I made no attempt to talk over the Ruthenian representatives. I simply put the case before them: you can join either us or the Hungarians or the Poles; it is for you to choose. They chose us. It was a long task, just as it was in Europe, to unite the smaller European nations in their fight for peace, to reach an agreement with Poles, Ruthenians, Serbs, Croats, Rumanians, and others as well; the result was the joint declaration of independence in Philadelphia. It remained for us to win over the American people, so there were meetings, consultations, lectures, and more or less ceremonious gatherings in meetings and congresses; but it was no use by itself; we had to work on public opinion which up to then knew little about us and still less about the Slovaks. In America it had been a popular war against the Germans, but the tangled national problems of Central Europe were quite strange to the people. Fortunately the Czechs in the United States had been carrying on a propaganda campaign against Austria ever since the beginning of the war; and then, when our legions in Siberia drew the attention of the whole world to themselves, we held victory in our hands. The chief thing was to lose no time, since war was already drawing to an end. As a matter of fact, it ended about six months sooner than I expected.

When public opinion had been prepared, I began to negotiate with American official circles, with

Lansing, Colonel House, and others; in these relations my old American friend, Mr. Crane, helped us a great deal. His son was Lansing's secretary. President Wilson I met, I think, four times. My first impression of him was one of such perfect *neatness*; I said to myself, it's obvious he has a wife who loves him. We understood each other fairly well—after all, we had both been professors. He was more obstinate in his principles, but he was willing to consider objections. He knew about me, and we had been in indirect contact before I came to America. I saw that he would not be at home in European affairs, and that his very directness would prevent him from understanding European statesmen; I warned him not to come to Europe to the Peace Conference, but he would not be persuaded. He was too keen on his plan for a League of Nations to think of difficulties.

In May 1918 my daughter Olga came from England to join me in America. It was during the time when boats were not allowed to carry women and children because of the submarine warfare, so she obtained a passage through an order from President Wilson that she was coming as his courier with despatches; she was the only woman in a convoy of eight ships. I lived most of the time in Washington, and I used to go riding on horseback in Rock Creek Park to get some air and exercise. As a matter of fact, it was there that I nearly broke my neck; I wanted to try jumping the highest obstacles. After that our people wouldn't let me ride alone. They bought me my first car; it was a little Dodge. I remember how we drove— or tried to drive—in it through the streets on Armistice Day. Such popular rejoicings I have never seen in my life; people were all shouting and singing, rushing into each other's arms, tooting on motor horns; the whole of New York was snowed under with confetti. We Czechs have not the art of being as wildly and childishly gay as the Americans.

When I received the telegram telling me that they had elected me President at home—well, I simply hadn't thought of it till then. When I had thought over what I would do after my return home, I had simply imagined myself a journalist. When I got the telegram I was merely worried— worried about my departure, who was to come with me, and so on. I sailed from America on November 20th, my wife's birthday. On the voyage I had my first moment of rest during these four years; I was able to play chess with my daughter —I haven't had a chessman in my hand since then. I used to walk up and down the deck watching the sea and thinking how it had all come about— and I was happy! We had managed it after all!

The Old Tree

One thing surprised me when I got home from the war, and that was that my friends, my contemporaries, had all got so old. During the whole of the war I had forgotten almost everything else, I was so engrossed in all its details and in its final outcome. When I saw this change in other people I realized with a shock that I must have grown old too!

Just look at that old oak tree yonder. It is said to be nine hundred years old; but see how strong it is, how full of life! Its great stature and even its great age do not prevent it from putting out new leaves and blossoming into new life. Men should grow old like that! It should be no great feat to live to a hundred years old—but we shan't attain this of course by artificial, unnatural means. To live healthily in fresh air and sun, eat and drink moderately, live morally, work with muscle, heart, and brain, have something to care for, an aim in life—that is the whole secret of longevity. And not to lose one's live interest; because interest is really life itself; without interest and without love there is no life.

We measure life by too one-sided a standard, simply by its length and not by its greatness. We think more of how we can lengthen life than how

284

we can fill it. Many people are afraid of death, but they take no account of the fact that they themselves and many others like them are really only living half a life, empty, loveless, without real happiness. By recognizing truth, by ordering our life morally, by loving actively, we can have a share of eternity in this life of ours, we can prolong our life not by days or years, but by eternity. It is good that we are trying to increase the length of man's life, but we must do more than that; we must increase its worth. There is a dream which often comes back to me—I don't know how I come to have it, perhaps it is a recollection of some picture—I see a ship on the sea and an angel bending over it with an hour-glass; and every now and then a drop runs down from the hour-glass into the sea, and the angel says "Another minute passed away." I always think of that dream as a warning: work, do something, while your minutes are passing.

Many people grow old simply because they are too comfortable and have no wish to do anything. Not to grow old does not mean merely lasting; it means to go on always growing, always improving; each year must be for a man like climbing one rung higher up a ladder. I watch myself carefully to see if I am growing older; I test my intellectual powers, my memory, my breadth, and quickness of grasp. As soon as I see that I am beginning to lose my mental power, I shall at once make room for someone younger.

*　　*　　*

If I had my way, I should try to get on without doctors; but if people do not know how to take care of their health themselves, then the medicos must look after it. A cultivated man will observe and consider his diet; that isn't materialism; materialism is thoughtless eating and drinking immoderately whatever one has a taste for, whether it is reasonable or not. So the first rule is moderation: to eat and drink a great deal less than folk usually do. If you want to know about myself I will tell you. I have three meals a day. For breakfast I first have fruit, then a shred of meat, toast and marmalade, or sometimes a piece of fried bacon, and half a glass of tea without sugar; I used sometimes to have a couple of soft-boiled eggs, but that is said not to be very healthy. For dinner I have a few spoonfuls of thick soup, a small piece of meat and plenty of vegetables, some kind of sweet, fruit, and black coffee. For supper I have got used to having just a plate of milk pudding or a piece of cake and a cup of milk with a dash of coffee in it. That is sufficient. Even my guests I don't overload with more than this for supper, except that as a concession they have an entrée

286

first, usually fish or something else light; it is supposed to stimulate the appetite; I don't see why that is necessary; it is enough if one satisfies one's natural hunger. Apart from these three meals I take nothing except perhaps a cup of tea at five o'clock if I have a guest. The stomach wants rest like any other working member of the body, and it gets it while we are fasting. Most people work their stomachs to death; over-eating is like carrying a heavy load beyond one's strength. Nowadays doctors are actually warning people against getting too fat; fat people don't live to a great age because they inflict far too much exertion on most of their organs. And besides that, fatness is not nice to see. It is all part of a humanitarian programme that people should be beautiful.

As for drinking, I have never in my life drunk spirits. Wine I have drunk from my boyhood; I was born in the wine country; beer I learned to drink when I came to the town. It was only just before I was fifty that I realized that alcohol is not beneficial but is actually bad, and I gave up drinking altogether. After my last illness the doctors forced me to drink a glass of wine before meals; I did not like it, and finally I found by experience that I got on as well without wine and even better. As President I even wanted to make my guests forgo wine or beer with their meals, but I didn't succeed.

Well, I thought, let's each do as we like. Temperance isn't my religion, but I sometimes try to make my fellow citizens see how terribly stupid drinking is.

For the rest my way of life is simple. When I get up in the morning I have a cold bath and then do my Sokol exercises. I have one or two hours' exercise on foot daily, or else I go riding; I can stand two to three hours in the saddle now, and up to a few years ago I could stand five. Cleanliness is important too—a clean mouth, clean teeth, a clean body, and clean breath. As for smoking, I smoked as a boy, playing at the man—it was in 1866, and I wanted to show the Prussians that I was a Czech, so I made cigarettes out of red, white, and blue paper and puffed at these in front of them. Later at the University I smoked for a time (what I enjoyed most really was rolling them deftly). Smoking, drinking, and intemperance are not needs, they are only habits. If we want to bring up healthy children, it is not enough to tell them what is healthy and what isn't; it is not enough to explain it to them; we need to breed healthy habits in them by practice. I have read somewhere that death is only a bad habit; I don't want to argue about death, but certainly premature old age and many illnesses are only bad habits. I believe that as time goes on we shall not only have more and more control over our natural strength but our health and habits too, so that we shall come to regard many of our present illnesses with the same horror as we now regard the plagues of the Middle Ages and of some parts of Asia. Modern medicine is right when it advocates not merely cure but prevention—and education.

Being a President

I was not at all prepared to be made President. Even though I was acknowledged as the head of our National Council abroad, and was certain that the outcome of the war for us would be revolution setting us free from Austria, I had not had time to think of what I should do myself when I got back home. Perhaps I should go on for a time as professor at the University, and perhaps side by side with that do some journalism and go into Parliament. When they elected me President at home in November 1918 I had no time to worry my head about it much, at the moment; I was too busy with everything that had to be done before I left America. It was only when I was on the boat that I had time to study the new situation. I compared the American and Swiss Republics; I examined the list of available persons with political and administrative experience; I thought out the details of the necessary machinery of State. I had worked for years on the

289

analysis of the State, its forms and functions; as a member of the Austrian Parliament I had studied the structure of Austria-Hungary in detail, and all the sources of its political and cultural strength. It was a considerable disadvantage to me that I did not know how things had been developing at home while I was away. And I had also to prepare myself for what would be happening in London, Paris, and Italy; I knew that I should have to visit those political centres and the persons who were going to make a new Europe at the Peace Conference. I thought about that a great deal. I even had to get accustomed to the formalities of being head of a State.

When I got back I was not feeling very well; I didn't think I had very much longer to live. Perhaps it was the result of all the exertions and excitements of the war and of the attacks of influenza that I had had. In my work I had to be on the look-out, as each case arose, to see that continuity was preserved and that nothing upset the work that we had been doing beyond the frontiers of our country. The thing to do was to secure the fruit of those years of work and negotiations abroad; that was my first care. At home I had to get accustomed to new conditions; the Government was already formed; there was a Revolutionary National Assembly, there were already some new laws and institutions. It was fortunate that I had known almost all the people in our political life for many years past, so that I knew what to expect of each of them. But there was a lot more; I had to learn something new almost every day. It is no small thing to be the first President of a new State, with no governmental and representative tradition. I saw mistakes made; I made some myself. One small detail for example: I forgot that I was a President and promised my friends that the day after taking the oath to the Constitution I would meet them at the café where we used to hold our political discussions in 1914. I went on foot from the Castle down into the town; of course the people flocked in huge crowds. So I learnt to be a President, and I'm still learning to-day; new situations keep arising about which I have to decide.

I had to think a great deal about what the President of a democratic State should be like. When the Constitution was made many people imagined that the function of President of the Republic would be more or less ornamental, without real power to influence political events. It was a strict analogy with the English constitutional monarchy; but our first Constitution was not ready for that, either in theory or practice. It took over the old machinery of State (and in this it was right) and made new machinery under the pressure of circumstances on the basis of changed conditions. I was able to make my influence felt, chiefly through the help of Švehla and a few other men; I saw to it that the President had the constitutional right not only to approve the Governmental and Parliamentary proposals before they become law, but to take part in Governmental Councils, and if need be even to take the initiative of suggesting measures to Parliament. I was also anxious to ensure the expert elements of the administration and Government; that is how we come to have a combination of parliamentary and expert government so that the leading officials of the State— Beneš and Švehla, for instance—continue in office.

I think our Constitution is a good one; but we had, and have still, to supplement the written word by experience. In our Constitution, as in every other, there are certain points which are not clear. Certain things might be different. For instance, we have a comparatively large number of Members of Parliament; according to the English model we could have done with two hundred. But to change a Constitution is a delicate business; look at the example of America where, in the hundred and forty years since the Constitution was framed in 1787, only nineteen amendments have been passed out of more than two thousand proposed. And these amendments are really supplements, for instance, the women's franchise; the original text remains in force. As I say, not only the letter of the law is important; what matters is the way in which we understand it and put it into practice. All laws, including the provisions of the Constitution, remain through the constitutional development of circumstances, but finally we see where amendments and new measures must be made. So-called customary law is not a thing of the past, belonging to the dawn of civilization; it still holds good, although in a different form.

In everything I have done I have had to consider what effect it was going to have on the shaping of precedent and custom, and that has often been very hard to decide. Our tradition has had to be consciously built up. Take the example of the indispensable ceremonial of State. I tried to make it an expression of democratic feeling answering to the needs of the times and the genius of our nation. I should have liked our people to realize the use of symbols better than before; not only religious but also political life finds its intellectual and imaginative expression in symbols. Until I became President I had lived as far as possible in seclusion, but since then I have had to reconcile myself to having these guards downstairs, and parades, receptions, and all the other ceremonies of office; I tell myself sometimes that it's all part of the job. As far as all this is concerned, I may say that we have done well;

the public ceremonial of our republic has been an example in many ways. For myself, I live as I should like every citizen to live: my only expensive hobby is my books, but they will be put at the service of the public.

The thing which I do feel as a really great hardship is that I am continuously under the eyes of my officials, and on public view.

Of course, political and administrative questions demanded a great deal of hard thought every day. Just think of the early days of our republic: the financial collapse all round us, the civil war and *coups d'état* in almost all the neighbouring States; we can scarcely remember now which danger seemed to threaten us most in those days—economic breakdown, or a wave of communism, or desperate attempts by the deposed classes of the old régime to overthrow the republic. One had to be on guard all the time against mistakes both old and new. To-day we almost take it as a matter of course that our State has survived all that in comparative peace, and through it all, built up our Constitution and our institutions, but all the same it meant hard thinking **and** not losing our heads. I had to have a conference every week and sometimes several times a week with Švehla, Tusar, Rašin, and the other leading men. Beneš was abroad so I had detailed correspondence with him. We had so many consultations, and then a meal together, that was another consultation in a different style, and walks together and more talks! I like to look back on that time; I realized clearly and concretely the value of personality in politics and in the State. A good programme is excellent as far as it goes; but besides that there must be an honest, courageous, and wise man, who has the courage of responsibility. That is why I always pay more attention to people than to slogans. We are too much given to slogans; I think it is one of our legacies from Austria-Hungary; under Austria it was not we who administered and governed but Vienna, so we got into an unhealthy habit of catch-words. I know that in politics you can't get on without a slogan; but now that we have our State in our own hands our slogans—or if you like our ideals—must be embodied in exact and well thought out demands and practical programmes. You see in our journalism (and in this I include the journalism of all countries) how *approximately* we think, inexactly, negatively, polemically, unconstructively. I am never against criticism; heavens, the greater part of my life I have been active as a critic! But I want criticism to be constructive, helpful, not excited. You know even a revolution can't be merely negative; it must have a positive preparation and basis; how, then, can negative criticism achieve reform?

PRESIDENT MASARYK TELLS HIS STORY

Of course I still have frequent conferences with our leading statesmen and ministers. I try to supervise everything, though I meddle with administrative procedure as little as possible; the Ministers must get their own experiences just as I had to get mine. Often, almost every day, I say to myself: thirty years more of peaceful, sensible, energetic development, and our State will be secure; but I can count on my fingers the real leaders, the men with strength and experience, who are to carry our country over these thirty years. The younger men, it is true, I hardly know. I am not looking merely for politicians but for statesmen, and of them, I will say frankly, we have not enough to succeed without very hard work. So we must be careful not to discard our proved workers without cause, and not to wear them out! We have to learn a great deal: in the first place, we must learn to judge our Members of Parliament, politicians, journalists, and officials by a higher standard of statesmanship. You are not a statesman if you do not see at least a bit of the way before you and prepare the development of the years to come.

Perhaps nothing is so important, either in politics or life, as to understand people, to recognize the real men who are truly capable but also to see through the false ones who without the justification of ability try to elbow their way to the front. Every successful revolution brings to the surface a number of parvenus, agitators, and false prophets. We have ours, too; by their fruits ye shall know them, and in the end you will know them all. In spite of everything that divides us into camps and parties we probably all want a sensible and honest policy, and even in politics twice two are and always will be four.

To my mind foreign policy has always been as important as home policy, and especially in the post-war period. There it is doubly necessary to look ahead and be prepared for coming events, never to be surprised by anything. Questions of the future are never very narrowly defined. We can only venture to make an agreement in advance when we have taken into account, within the limits of possibility, the widest connections and the interrelation of all the forces and agents. We must know in order to foresee, as Comte says. Foreign policy is and should be a great thing, and an important national and world idea. All the same, few people realize how much spade work and unseen effort a real foreign policy demands. For me, at any rate, it is an unceasing labour; I convinced myself during the war of the practical value in politics, especially international politics, of personal relations, and honest personal information. Sympathy and confidence are a better argument than any amount of cunning. So you see in that field the function of a President is sometimes formally official but far more often private; of course I know quite well that the idea of privacy in this case is not legally defined. And because our people have little contact with countries abroad we still need to keep forging informative and friendly links with the innumerable people who come to us out of interest in our State and our institutions. Few people know how much time I have devoted to this. Many people come to see me not as President but as the author of books and studies, political and otherwise, in which they are interested; so in my intercourse with them I am able to build up relations as writer, professor, and journalist. I am not fond of talking and expounding; I prefer to listen, but whether I like it or not I must give information in return. Good friendly relations with foreign countries make possible suitable economic intercourse.

Another chapter of my policy is the Castle—I mean the alterations and additions. I want to make it a monument of our history, a portrait of our old-new State, a symbol not only of the past but of the future—in fact to transform a royal into a democratic Castle.

From the outset I have given a lot of attention to our army; I studied military matters while still a member of the Austrian Parliament, and much

298

more intensively in war-time, when I had to calculate the outcome of the war and was organizing our Corps in Russia. I am a convinced pacifist—but I love the army! Even when there are no more wars the two fundamental points of soldierly honour, discipline and courage, will always be useful to every man. I want peace, but that does not mean that I am going to meet aggression unarmed; rather the contrary. I want practical not Utopian peace; that means that I exert all the power of my brain and all my love of my nation and humanity to keep the peace; but also, if necessary, to make war. So let's be brave and manly and as strong as we can be. There has never been the slightest contradiction between my humanitarianism and my activities in the defence of the State. We need peace in order to build up our State, and for the personal happiness of us all; that is why we must all work for a durable and well-ordered peace. And all the other States and nations need peace just as much as we do. The new Europe is like a laboratory built over the great graveyard of the world war, a laboratory which needs the work of all. And democracy—modern democracy—is in its infancy. It would be a mistake to shut our eyes to the adherents and exponents of the old aristocratic and monarchic order of things who are also at work.

It may be that we shall always have armies,

though perhaps in another form; certainly we shall have them for a long time yet; what I mean is, a nation needs a trained body of efficient, hardy young men ready to be sent at a moment's notice to work on the scene of accidents and catastrophies and for purposes of defence.

A more difficult question for me was that of capital punishment. There have been many days when I have had to sign a death-warrant, and nights when I have had to think it over; I have marked them on my calendar with a black cross. I have followed carefully to see whether capital punishment has an effect on crime; I have studied the statistics of crime, and especially of murder, all my life, but I do not see that the death penalty has had a deterrent effect on evildoers; at the moment of committing a murder the murderer does not think of the penalty but of the success of his deed. The most definite effect is on the rest of the citizens, especially on their way of thinking. My argument for the death penalty is not that it is a deterrent, but that there is in it a moral expiation: to take a man's life is such a frightful wrong that it can only be expiated by an equally heavy ransom. I make, of course, a proper distinction between murder and homicide, and I recognize extenuating circumstances in the case of every criminal, as modern criminal psychology demands; but in exceptional circumstances I

300

cannot refute the argument that capital punishment is in harmony with the metaphysical consideration of the value of human life. I believe and hope that it will be abolished with the consent of all, as people become more moral and civilized.

*
* *

You ask me what I consider as the culminating point of my life; I would say my election to the presidency and the fact that I am able to shoulder this burden as a great honour and an equally solemn duty. My personal satisfaction, if I may call it so, lies deeper: for as the head of the State I relinquish nothing that I believed in and loved as a penniless student, a carping critic, a reforming politician; occupying a position of power, I do not seek for myself any other moral law or relationship to my fellow men, to the nation, and the world than those which guided me before. I may say that office confirms and completes everything that I have believed, so that I have not needed to change one item of my faith in humanity and in democracy, in the search for truth, nor in the supreme moral and religious command to love men. I can still affirm from experience which I am continually acquiring that the same moral and ethical rule applies to the State, and those who administer it, as to the individual. This does not spring from satisfaction that

301

through all my life, with its strange vicissitudes and changes, I have remained myself; it is more important that the human and social ideals which I confessed have endured and become acknowledged through all those trials. I can tell myself that in that incessant struggle for a better nation and people I was on the right side. That conviction is enough to make a man's life beautiful and happy.